The Other Idahoans

Forgotten Stories of the Boise Valley

INVESTIGATE BOISE COMMUNITY RESEARCH SERIES
BOISE STATE UNIVERSITY
2016

VOL. 7

The Investigate Boise Community Research Series
publishes fact-based essays of popular scholarship
concerning the problems and values that shape
metropolitan growth.

Todd Shallat, *editor*

Colleen Brennan, *managing editor*

Molly Humphreys, *research associate*

Toni Rome, *graphic designer*

Corey Cook, *dean of School of Public Service*

BOISE STATE UNIVERSITY
School of Public Service
1910 University Drive – MS 1900
Boise, ID 83725
tshalla@boisestate.edu
(208) 761-0485
sps.boisestate.edu/publications

BOISE STATE UNIVERSITY

About the cover: A fallen angel glows in the orange light of a Boise bordello. Frontispiece: William "Doc" Hison at his Snake River homestead. Opposite: Idaho children on a New Deal farm resettlement project, 1936. Next: Riding the rails, 1935.

Generous support was provided by the Patricia Herman Fund and Professor Emeritus Errol D. Jones.

ISBN: 978-0-9907363-4-9

2016

Contents

Preface

An antique tractor swings from a crane into the bowels of the 7-acre Simplot compound rising between Myrtle and Front streets in downtown Boise. Jack's Urban Meeting Place, or JUMP, features 52 turn-of-the-century tractors; also classrooms, roof gardens, an amphitheater, a recording studio, a dance studio, and a five-story tubular slide. Only once, in the lobby, does JUMP tribute its founder, but J. R. Simplot is ever-present. Jack's tractors recall the agrarian roots of Idaho's industrialization. JUMP also embodies the American romance of farm boys from humble beginnings who made more money than they knew how to spend.

JUMP's crane shadows the freight yard where risk-takers of another sort once labored for the Oregon Short Line. Young men from Japan who emigrated via Hawaii slept in company boxcars. To the south near the river's floodplain were blacks and dark Europeans in a "colored town" of Jim Crow housing. Nearby, along Front and Grove, were flophouses that boarded young women abandoned by spouses and boyfriends. Mothers with infants found cots in the county poor farms. Others became sex workers in Levy's Alley in saloons like the Bucket of Blood. Soundless, faceless, their backstreets lost to high-rise hotels and banks, they were Boiseans too common to be seen from the towers.

"All things, it is said, are duly recorded . . . but not quite," said Harlem's Ralph Ellison in a 1952 novel about socially invisible men. "What did they [the historians] ever think of us transitory ones? . . . Birds of passage who were too obscure for learned classification, too silent for the most sensitive recorders of sound?"

Admittedly it is hard to track misfortune. *Boise: An Illustrated History* (2000), the standard text, pictures an Athens emerging from sagebrush—vibrant, inclusive, polite. Fully a third of the book is a tribute to business leaders. Likewise, in Carol MacGregor's 2006 study of the frontier city, "charity" and "capitalist values" made Boise a prosperous hub. No matter the hostility to organized labor and tax-funded social programs. Class bias disconnects the culture of wealth from the plight of the bottom rung.

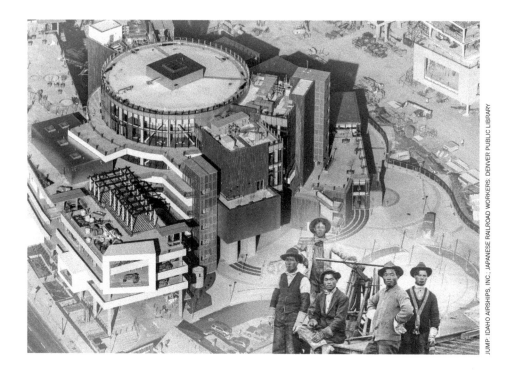

The Other Idahoans tells alternative stories. Each essay features a hard-labor location: a poor farm, a graveyard, a prison camp, a prison ward, a gold mine, a farm community, and a grid of minority housing. We close with an underside driving tour of 24 historic places. All worthy of landmark status, they are lessons at odds with the fables that wealth inspires.

In the shadow of Simplot. JUMP rises over the rail yards where immigrants from Japan laid track for the Oregon Short Line.

Todd Shallat, Ph.D.
Center for Idaho History and Politics
Boise State University
March 2016

1 | Boise's Forgotten Pandemic

Headstones mark the city's deadliest virus.

by Mistie Rose

The Great Pandemic of 1918 spread through a fatal cough. Vomiting and delirium followed. Victims spat blood, then suffocated. Most died within 24 hours.

Known as the Spanish flu—elsewhere as the Spanish Lady, the Blue Death, the Fever of War, and the Great Influenza—the killer may have originated in China as a lethal strain of H1N1 influenza. Or it may have begun as bird or swine flu in Kansas, where the flu was first diagnosed. Shifting and drifting with genetic mutation, the influenza devastated the killing fields of Europe at the close of World War I. By October 1918, it had swept the globe from France to New Zealand. By February 1919, when suddenly the phantom vanished, the wartime epidemic had killed more soldiers than died under enemy fire.

Epidemiologists have estimated that a third of the Earth's population may have been exposed to the airborne infection. Perhaps 1 in every 200 people died after exposure.

Wartime suspicion clouded every aspect of the Great Pandemic. How did it kill? Where was it born? Cures were also elusive. Doctors worldwide were slow to acknowledge the devastation. The Red Cross could do little more than provide surgical masks to swaddles faces in cotton gauze.

Doctors in Idaho were as dumbfounded as any. "I myself came down with the disease in January 1919," said Leonard J. Arrington, a historian raised in Twin Falls. "Every hamlet was stricken," he continued. "Every neighborhood lost children, parents, and grandparents. Almost everyone old enough to have memories of it recalls with grief the passing of a relative, a friend, a respected official."

Sadly, few records exist for Ada County. In 1919, when federal health officials conducted an influenza census, Boise was outside its scope. In 1920, Ada was one of 22 Idaho counties that frustrated health officials by failing to tally and carefully label causes of death by infectious disease.

Perhaps the worst of the fever bypassed Boise. Or perhaps in the Boise Valley, where nostalgia clouded misfortune, the trauma was subconsciously blocked for a city's

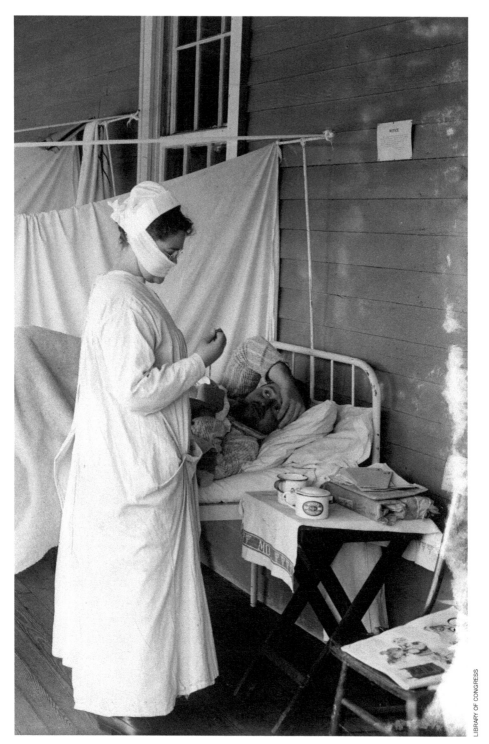

self-preservation. Perhaps it called into question the fables of frontier progress with memories too horrific not to repress.

Origins of the Pandemic

Was it meningitis? Bacteria pneumonia? A plot hatched by Germany's Bayer aspirin? A virus launched from a U-boat?

Europeans first scapegoated Spain because Spanish newspapers had been quick to report the story. But it was an epidemic like no other. Tamer strains of viral influenza had long been common in Europe, hitting mostly the poor, the very old, and the very young. But the 1918 pandemic was more democratic. It crippled men as powerful as FDR and President Woodrow Wilson, and the virus hit young adults especially hard.

President Woodrow Wilson contracted the flu in April 1919.

Scientists still debate why the flu became so deadly. Not until 2004 were microbiologists able to isolate the murderous H1N1 strain. Some say the virus, born in China, had been transmitted through the wartime migrants who labored behind British lines. Some say the fatal strain had mutated in the filth of field hospitals and troop ships. Others say the influenza was American born.

Camp Funston, a military camp in Ft. Riley, Kansas

The killer, whatever its source, savaged the United States in three murderous waves: the first, in the early spring of 1918; the second, in the fall of 1918; the third, in the winter of 1918-1919. "Patient zero" was said to have been Albert Gitchell, an army cook from Kansas, the first to be diagnosed. On the morning of March 11, 1918, at Camp Funston in Ft. Riley, Kansas, Gitchell staggered into the infirmary with a fever of 103° F. By midday the camp was flooded with 107 cases. By month's end, the number of cases had surged to 1,127. Forty-eight victims died.

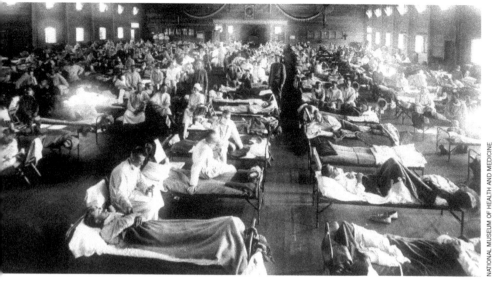

Doctors at first shrugged it off as germs spread by dust storms. In September 1918, however, when the virus jumped to New England, the pandemic could not be ignored. Surgeon General of the U.S. Army Victor Vaughan reported the trauma from Camp Devens outside of Boston on the day 63 soldiers died. "The faces soon wear a bluish cast," said Vaughan, reporting the horror; "a distressing cough brings up the blood stained sputum. In the morning the dead bodies are stacked about the morgue like cord wood." Doctors were entirely helpless. Vaughan feared that the killer might murder every human on Earth.

Patients at Camp Funston

Death toll estimates vary. The U.S. Department of Health has estimated that 165,000 Americans died of the influenza. Ghana in West Africa may have lost 100,000 people; Brazil, 300,000; Japan, 390,000. Worldwide estimates range from 20 to 100 million. The influenza killed more people in 24 months than HIV-AIDS has killed in 35 years.

Idaho and the Boise Valley

"When your head is blazing, burning / And your brain within is turning / Into buttermilk from churning / It's the Flu," wrote a poet in Idaho Falls. "When your stomach grows uneasy / quaking, querulous, and queasy / All dyspeptic and diseasy / It's the Flu."

Cod liver oil was commonly prescribed as a remedy for influenza.

U.S. NATIONAL LIBRARY OF MEDICINE

As the disease spread and the death toll rose, the government distributed pamphlets and advertisements to educate the public.

Boise doctors remained unconcerned through the summer of 1918. Dr. William Brady, the *Statesman*'s medical columnist, predicted the virus would be no worse than others that regularly crossed the Atlantic. "Avoid worry," said another physician. Westerners were said to be hardy enough to stand tall against influenza. And people who lived in cities, it was said, had resistance to diseases spread in a crowd. Fresh air and exercise were recommended. A Boise Rexall drugstore prescribed a flu regimen of iron pills, hydrogen peroxide, antiseptic gargle, and cod liver oil.

Tunnel vision on the war in Europe kept the disease from Boise's headlines. "FRENCH TROOPS HOLD OFF HUNS" was the *Statesman* headline on October 2, 1918, when the flu struck Caldwell and Star. Fifteen people from six families had visited with an infected friend from Missouri. All were quarantined after reporting dangerous symptoms. Olive Shawver of N. 22nd Street had the sad misfortune of being the City of Boise's first reported victim. On October 15, she was confined to her North End home.

By mid-October the mayor of Boise had joined the Red Cross and the U.S. Public Health Service to ban meetings in public places, closing churches, theaters, pool halls, dance halls, courtrooms, cigar shops, and funeral homes. Boise schools mostly stayed open. In Kimberly, Idaho, however, city officials refused to let Boise-bound travelers step off the train. Deputies in Custer County guarded the mountain passes, arresting travelers or turning them back at gunpoint.

Idaho's Native Americans grieved some of the pandemic's worst devastation. In 1918, of the 4,200 natives in Idaho, there were 650 documented cases of flu. Seventy-five died from flu-related heart failure and suffocation. In Nez Perce, a town of about 600 on the tribe's reservation, health officials estimated 300 cases.

Mormon communities received aid from Utah when the third wave materialized. The city of Paris in Bear Lake County, Idaho, may have lost as many as 500 people—a mortality rate of 50%.

Boise, meanwhile, was ill-equipped as any western city. Boise's Red Cross offered $75 per month and all travel expenses to lure experienced nurses. Gloves on their hands, gauze on their faces, the nurses delivered hot meals from sanitary community kitchens. Trolley conductors with police power had orders to prevent passengers from spitting or placing their feet on the seats.

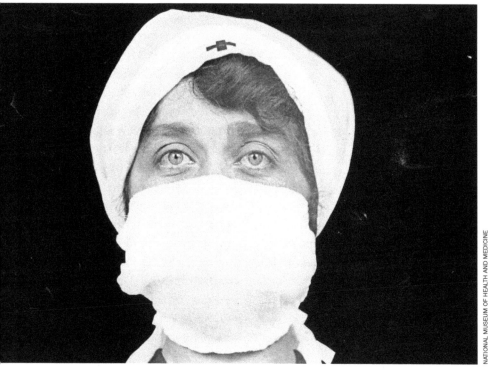

Red Cross nurse

Tunnel vision on the war in Europe continued to dominate Boise headlines through October of 1918 as Germany capitulated. On November 11, 1918, Armistice Day, Boiseans flooded the Idaho Statehouse to hear Governor Moses Alexander proclaim America's moment of triumph. A parade—fever-be-damned—erupted on Boise's Main Street. "Ten thousand yelling, shooting, screeching, tooting, rooting, laughing, talking citizens of Boise parade the streets," the *Statesman* reported. A band played "Hot Time in the Old Town Tonight." A small boy milked laughs with a sign: "The Kaiser has got the flu. He has flown." The flu, aside from that sign, seemed to be largely forgotten. No health department official dared to stop the celebration. The *Statesman* reported that only one Boisean at the victory party had worn a surgical mask.

No one remembers whether or not the parade spread the infection. Medical records are sketchy. Brigham Young University has since compiled a "death index" of Idaho fatalities. From October through February, 1918-1919, the index reports 279 deaths in Boise. Influenza or flu is listed as the cause of death in 75 of those cases, more than half of them young adults. Flu-like pneumonia is listed as a cause of death in 60 additional cases.

But if Boise followed the pattern of other American cities, the pandemic of 1918 was dangerously underreported. Hospitals often refused to admit what seemed to be mild cases. And because the virus came in waves with evermore deadly mutations, there was no standard diagnostic test.

Local resentment of state officials may have also blurred the reporting. On October 20, 1918, for example, state health officials denounced "unpatriotic" physicians who refused to keep careful statistics. One of the accused was Dr. George Collister, the founder of a subdivision. Officials alleged that Collister had failed to quarantine 32 Basques in their Grove Street rooming house. In 1920, the state's Department of Public Welfare reported in frustration that half of Idaho's counties had refused to fill out reports.

And then, inexplicably, the virus subsided. In January 1919, even as influenza rebounded elsewhere, state legislators returned to Boise to ratify the Eighteenth Amendment, prohibiting the sale and consumption of alcohol. Theaters had already reopened and, on January 19, the *Statesman* headlined "SCHOOLS FREE OF DISEASE." Boise flu cases had fallen below 600. By February the phantom was gone.

Grave Misfortunes

No memorial recalls Boise's pandemic—none but the granite in the cemeteries, marking the victims in rows. Boise's cemetery at Morris Hill inters at least 110 bodies from the wartime virus. Laborers, housekeepers, nurses, cooks, janitors,

Dr. George Collister

and railroad workers—they were local victims of global misfortune, more than half of them young adults.

Agnes Stites was one of these victims. Age 22 when she died in 1918, Stites suffocated while spitting blood at St. Alphonsus Hospital. Her flu-stricken baby daughter, age 22 months, died the following day.

Ystora Yoshihara of Japan, another victim of influenza, was a naturalized citizen who worked as a cook at the OK Restaurant on Boise's Main Street. Influenza took him at age 41.

Albert P. Smith of Boise, age 50, died from influenza and heartbreak just 4 days after the death of his teenage daughter, Thelma Louise. He had been a boiler inspector in the Eastman Building. She had worked as a stenographer.

Edward Jeff Brummett, a farmer, had relocated from New Mexico with his wife and children about 6 months before his death by influenza at St. Luke's Hospital. His wife also died of the influenza. He was 28. She was 20. Their daughter and son took sick but survived.

Headstone of Edward Brummet, one of 110 people who fell victim to the pandemic

What these unfortunates had in common was bad timing, mostly. Bad timing had made them too young for immunities from past pandemics, too old to benefit from the advances in medical science that brought virus vaccines. Bad timing, moreover, had brought these victims to Boise at the fluke tragic moment when 12,000 Idaho troops returned from Europe jubilation, spewing disease.

A century later it remains our own sad modern misfortune to write about common people in an era of celebrity wealth. "Sad stories are a hard sell in Boise," says Bruce DeLaney, co-owner of Rediscovered Books in downtown Boise. Only the headstones are left to recall forgotten pandemics, marking memories collectively lost.

MISTIE ROSE is a native of Boise and a graduate of Boise State University. Currently, she is pursuing a graduate degree in bioregional planning and urban design. She is married with two children and resides in northwest Boise.

Todd Shallat and Molly Humphreys contributed to this chapter.

2 | Dollar a Day

Mobs rioted against Japanese workers on the Oregon Short Line.

by Julie Okamura

Tadashichi Tanaka swam into the Seattle shore in 1885, dripping wet clothes hanging from his exhausted figure. It was called "smuggling in" or "jumping ship." Men left their ships while anchored in the port, never to see Japan again. Seaman Tadashichi Tanaka was one of many men who reached America in this way. Clever but illiterate, Tanaka came to America to make as much money as possible. Working as a contractor, he brought Japanese men to Idaho in October 1891 to work as railroad laborers. In doing so, Tanaka played a prominent role in the story of Japanese who came to the Boise Valley at the turn of the 19th century.

In May 1869, the first transcontinental railroad was completed, connecting Council Bluffs, Iowa, to Sacramento, California. Thousands of Chinese laborers undertook the hazardous task of building the Pacific line, from Sacramento to Promontory, Utah. By 1882, anti-Chinese sentiment had peaked as the economy experienced a downturn, resulting in the Chinese Exclusion Act. Railroads continued to expand across the western states and the demand for laborers outdrove the local supply. The U.S. government began recruiting men from Japan. Later, Tanaka would recruit men to come to Idaho.

At its closest point, Boise was still about 250 miles from the railroad in Kelton, Utah. Both goods and passengers traveled in wagons for the last grueling stage of the trip. Although Boise lagged behind other western cities in population, at less than 2,000 citizens, its residents campaigned for a railroad for decades before the Oregon Short Line finally made its way through Idaho in 1882 and 1883. The Oregon Short Line ran from Granger, Wyoming, and stopped at Huntington, Oregon. Unfortunately for Boiseans, the line went south of Boise, following an easier grade through Nampa.

Boiseans spent the next 10 years campaigning for a rail line into Boise. The next step included a line from Kuna to the Boise Bench, south of town, near the depot today, built by Mormon workers in 1887. Finally, in 1893, the Boise City Railroad and Terminal Company, a subsidiary of the Oregon Short Line, built the first stub line into downtown Boise.

Like many Japanese immigrants, Tanaka first lived in Seattle, unemployed and unfamiliar with the American way of life. Most likely, he hung about the Japanese section of town, frequenting gambling and prostitution houses. After living in the United States for 5 years, even men who jumped ship were allowed to obtain a "formal certificate of residence" from the Japanese Consulate. Eventually Tanaka left Seattle for Ogden (Utah), taking a Japanese prostitute with him. Once in Ogden, Tanaka met a Chinese labor subcontractor, known as Ah-Say, or Arthur. Arthur became infatuated with Tanaka's prostitute-girlfriend. In exchange for the woman, Arthur allowed Tanaka to subcontract under him in Idaho.

LIBRARY OF CONGRESS

A Prussian spire marked Boise's passenger depot.

When Tanaka arrived in Idaho, the city of Nampa had just been incorporated. Eight years earlier, the Oregon Short Line arrived and now Nampa was evolving into more than just a stop on the rail line. Tanaka set up an employment agency and hired 40 to 50 Japanese workers from Portland. Tanaka used connections in California, Oregon, and Washington to bring more Japanese workers to Idaho. By 1892, Tanaka had bypassed Arthur and worked directly under William Remington, a white contractor based out of Ogden. He sent 500 men from his base in Nampa to various places throughout Idaho to build and repair rail lines.

Working and Living Conditions

Railway section crews worked 10 hours a day. Japanese laborers often performed the most difficult jobs and under white supervisors. They were also paid less than white laborers regardless of their job. Whereas white railroad laborers earned $1.45 a day, Japanese men made $1.15 and sometimes as little as $1.00 a day. But the amount that ended up in their pockets was even less. Unscrupulous contractors such as Tanaka subtracted fees from the workers' wages. Tanaka took 10 cents a day from each worker as his own fee, a monthly "translation office fee" of $1 a month, and 50 cents a month for the medical clinic.

The medical clinic in Nampa, built in 1892, was Tanaka's idea. Its purpose was to care for the growing number of workers who were often ill or injured on the job. (Today in Nampa's Kohlerlawn Cemetery, headstones—some with three names each—mark the graves of Japanese railroad laborers.) Tanaka imposed an initial charge of $5 and then 50 cents per month from each man. These charges paid for the building and maintenance of the clinic. Tanaka also held part of their salary, at their request, to send to their families in Japan. Being a subcontractor, Tanaka was required to share his commission with the white regional contractor, William Remington. A year later, in 1893, Tanaka had about 500 men working for him. Many were recruited directly from Japan, primarily from Hiroshima, Wakayama, and Okayama prefectures.

NATIONAL PARK SERVICE

Workmen borrowed suits and retouched photos to lure "picture brides" from Japan.

As more men began leaving Japan, the Japanese government diligently worked at keeping men like Tanaka out of the United States because they gave Japan and its people a bad name. Japan watched the problems of China's immigrants and vigorously worked to separate themselves from the negative stereotypes and prejudice associated with the Chinese. Immigrant guide books soon popped up to assist the men and women in what to expect once they arrived in America. One warned men of "corrupt bosses," referring to railroad contractors.

Tanaka was aware of the negative consequences of being lumped with the Chinese. He helped his workers adapt and assimilate into Idaho culture by insisting they wear American clothes and eat American food. This type of assimilation, called *gaimentaki dōka* in Japanese, included observing American traditions such as not working on the Sabbath and commemorating American holidays such as Thanksgiving and Independence Day. Japanese associations in Idaho even entered floats in Fourth of July parades.

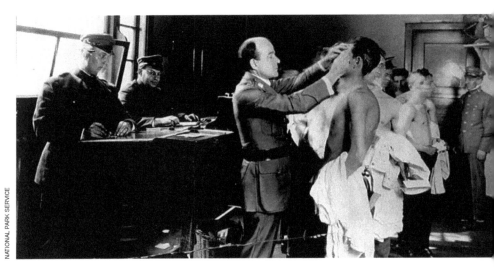

Japanese immigrants pass through immigration at Angel Island, about 1910.

In addition to making his men wear western shirts and pants, Tanaka prohibited them from eating rice, miso soup, and soy sauce. He told them, "Since you are different from Chinese, live like Americans!" In yet another way to stuff his pockets with money from his workers, Tanaka owned a restaurant near his office. He also sold food that came in on the Oregon Short Line. But his workers didn't know what to do with their limited American food items. They settled for cooking dumpling soup for breakfast and dinner. "We chopped bacon and fried it, then added potatoes and onions with salted water, and cooked the flour dumplings in that," one Japanese laborer told an interviewer decades later.

On cold and wintry nights,
Sound of the boiling kettle
Of dumpling soup–blub, blub...

(Taro)

The men took turns preparing meals for their section. If food costs rose above $3 or $4 a month for each person, the workers complained. The drive to spend as little as possible on food so they had more money to support their families cost some men their lives and many their health. One gentleman said, "Those who had left their families in Japan had the single-minded purpose of saving 1,000 yen in 3 years, without eating or drinking, and then go back to Japan." One laborer described it as "fasting for three years." Some of the men suffered from night blindness resulting from their poor diets. Among the Japanese graves in Kohlerlawn Cemetery in Nampa lie two men, Tashima Otomats and H. Kimura, who died in 1892, most likely due to their poor diets.

The housing provided by the railroad was next to the train tracks. It usually consisted of box cars or shacks, neither of which protected the workers from the heat or the cold. Six or eight men to a boxcar is how the men lived while laying track in the Boise Valley.

Negative Press and Xenophobia

Although the men were known for being hard workers and well behaved in camp, an 1892 article in the *Idaho Statesman* noted the arrival of more Japanese laborers contracted by "Tanaker" [sic] and their disorderly conduct. By summer of 1892, anxiety was building. As Japanese laborers continued arriving in Nampa, their presence caused uneasiness among the local citizens. Tensions grew. Some locals believed the men were competing and taking jobs away from white laborers. "The Japanese have within the last four months completely demoralized the laboring interests of Southern Idaho," reported the *Statesman*. In early July, Tanaka sent a section crew of a dozen Japanese workers to Mountain Home. When the townspeople found out, "about eighty *best* citizens" including "men of position" forced the crews out and demolished the newly constructed "shanty." The mob ordered the workers to leave on the first train.

At the end of July, a smallpox scare proved enough for citizens of Nampa, Caldwell, Notus, and Boise to force all the Japanese laborers out of the valley. The cause of the trouble

Chinese exclusion in the 1880s open the door for a limited quota of Japanese.

Steam locomotives reached beyond Boise to Barber in 1906.

was one sick Japanese man traveling to Portland on the train. Except for Tanaka (who was in Portland at the time), all of the Japanese railroad workers were ordered out of Nampa and sent to a "vacant building two miles north of town and an armed guard was placed over them." Boise warned the public of smallpox-exposed Japanese sneaking into town and expelled them from the capital city. A "committee of citizens" ran the Japanese out of Caldwell at 1 a.m. one morning. The *Caldwell Tribune* commented that the smallpox scare was reason enough to oust every Japanese in the county, including any Chinese. Another article stated Caldwell citizens were divided over the problem. "The more conservative condemn the action as an outrage, while others believe the proper thing was done."

"The Short Line will not again permit them to come into our midst," the article concluded.

Despite the prejudice and the calls to expel the Japanese, the demand for their labor continued. White laborers either quit at harvest time or were unwilling to work for such small wages. Because of recruiting offices set up in the Northwest, Hawaii, and Japan, hiring Japanese was easy and convenient. But opposition to Japanese laborers in Idaho continued. The *Idaho Statesman* reported from the Ada County Democratic convention platform, which stated, "We are opposed to the importation of foreign contract labor whether white or yellow, and we denounce the wholesale employment of servile Japanese on the Union Pacific Railroad as an outrage upon our laboring classes."

Boise Stub Line and River Bridge

The next spring, Tanaka sent groups of up to 12 men throughout Idaho to build and repair rail lines. Seventeen-year-old Inota Tawa was excited to leave his family's small farm in Okayama Prefecture and come to the United States. Poverty prevailed in Japan, especially in rural areas. One of his reasons for leaving, besides the adventure, was the opportunity to earn much more than if he stayed in Japan. In 1893, $1 was equal to 2 yen. Tawa had a goal of sending 1,000 yen back to his father in 3½ years.

The exchange rate for the U.S. dollar in 1893 yielded twice as many Japanese yen.

Tanaka also sent men to begin constructing the 6.3-mile stub line into downtown Boise. This would be the first line to bring passengers and freight directly into Boise. The Boise City Railroad and Terminal Company, controlled by Union Pacific, was chartered on March 20, 1893. Grading began on the stub line from the Boise Branch at Boise Junction into downtown on April 25. The *Statesman* kept track of the progress for residents. The workers built the 6-mile line in less than 4 months and the bridge in about 12 days.

Bridging the Boise River included not only driving pilings into the bank but also building up the banks with large lava boulders to prevent erosion. It took three men to move one rock—two men lifted the boulder onto the back of a third man and together they loaded the rock onto a flatcar. The flatcar then took the rocks to the river's edge, where the action was repeated in reverse and the rocks were placed on the bank. It was dangerous work. At least two Japanese laborers died from accidents on the job: J. Mizoguchi died on May 6, 1893, and N. Okita on May 20. Both were from Hiroshima Prefecture and were probably recruited directly from Japan.

Wooden trestles bridged Idaho's fractured landscapes.

On August 17, 1893, the first train made its way into downtown Boise, crossing the newly constructed wooden bridge. "It was greeted with cheers from the men, waving of handkerchiefs by the ladies, and music by the band," the *Idaho Statesman* reported. Although the train went into Boise and then had to back out, it was a monumental achievement for the small capital of Idaho. The newspaper made no mention of the Japanese laborers who graded the land, laid the tracks, and built the bridge across the Boise River.

In an event known as the Idaho Anti-Corruption Incident, Tadashichi Tanaka was accused of embezzlement when he could not account for $15,000 that his workers gave him for remittance to their families. Remington fired Tanaka and replaced him with another Japanese subcontractor, named Yasuteru Narita. The money was never found, but Tanaka reportedly "ended up living like a king" on 75 acres of land he had bought.

The contributions of Japanese railroad laborers have often been overlooked in the building of the Boise Valley. Their willingness to work on difficult and dangerous crews improved the valley and brought opportunities to the area that otherwise would have been slower in coming. Some of these men returned to Japan to fight in the Sino-Russian War, a few returned with their fortunes, but many stayed in the United States. After a few years, many of these men moved away from grueling railroad work and begin working on the sugar beet farms. Shortly thereafter, Issei (first-generation Japanese immigrants) began farming on their own. Because men were continually leaving the railroad but railroad construction continued, the demand for more laborers persisted until the Gentleman's Agreement in 1907 effectively stopped the immigration of Japanese laborers.

By 1905, one of six Japanese immigrants worked on railroads. The 1900 census includes 200 Japanese men living at the same address in Ada County; all are listed as railroad laborers. In Nampa, some of the men were grouped in sections of 10 to 12. At another area, the census taker specified that the men lived in box cars. Tatusgero Motonari was listed as a labor agent on Bannock Street. Subcontractors and their men were dispersed throughout Idaho and the Boise Valley. By 1907, there were about 1,500 Japanese men working throughout Idaho, constructing and repairing railroads.

The wooden Boise River bridge that the Japanese laborers built in 1893 was replaced 30 years later with a steel bridge that still stands in 2016. The bridge is on a section of the greenbelt just west of the connector and east of the Fallen Firefighters Memorial on Shoreline Drive. Pedestrians, bicyclists, and joggers cross this bridge each day with no awareness of its significance. The bridge is a reminder of the long forgotten Japanese who sacrificed their dreams, their health, and, in some cases, their lives to bring the railroad to downtown Boise.

A steel bridge, now part of the Boise River Greenbelt, marks the location of the original Boise River Bridge built by Japanese laborers in 1893.

JULIE OKAMURA is a graduate student in history at Boise State University, currently writing her thesis on first- and second-generation Japanese in Idaho. She is a native Idahoan who lives in Middleton. She enjoys spending time with her growing family, gardening, and reading.

3 | Unfit for Habitation

Paupers and the elderly labored at the county's poor farm.

by Namanny Asmussen

There was not enough water and soap in all of Boise to cleanse the stench of the county's poor farm. So said health inspector J. K. White in his 1915 indictment of Ada County's indigent care. The dilapidated farm north of Collister Station was "positively unfit for human habitation." Horrid, squalid, and invested with vermin, the farm was "disgraceful," even "criminal." White insisted that no one would voluntarily go there except as a last resort to cling to the last thread of life.

The condemnation cut deep into a city's genteel sense of itself as progressively modern. High-minded Boise in 1915 had an electric trolley and, upriver, the world's tallest dam. It had ballparks, opera houses, a symphony, a Carnegie library, and a palatial Moorish resort with geothermal spas. Charitable institutions included the Old Soldiers Home and the Children's Home orphanage on Warm Springs Avenue. But the city had no flophouse for transient shelter—nothing beyond the trackside camps for hobos and the drunk tank in the county jail. Its poorhouse was really a workhouse where the elderly and feeble-minded were given a cot and expected to farm.

The farm grew wheat and hay on 160 acres off the Farmers Union Canal where Dry Creek drained the foothills. A rustic ward of indigent men had a single reeking outhouse. A detached building housed the farm's superintendent and staff. The "inmates" were the diseased, the crippled, the detached, and the dislocated. Racially mixed, women and men, they were mothers nursing infants, abused children, the blind, the crippled, and the feeble-minded—never numbering more than 30—misfortunates lost in the blur between rural and urban in a society without clear distinctions between the senile and the raving mad. Yet the stories remain mostly hidden. Historian Arthur Hart, writing for the *Idaho Statesman*, found only fragments in the public record and no clear understanding of the institution's demise.

Still there remain fragments enough in the public record to question civic myths about Boise's abundance. One is the myth of visionary capitalism; another, the fable that charitable associations made Boise a neighborly place. Historian Carol MacGregor has

cited charity and capitalism as the social gospel that allowed early Boise to "prosper in isolation." But not every citizen prospered. For the disabled and elderly poor, lost in the city's shame and confusion, out-of-sight became out-of-mind.

Origins of Ada's Poor Farm

Public welfare in Ada County dates from the era of the Boise gold rush. In 1864 an act of the territorial legislature had vested Idaho counties with the care of paupers. Ada County became one of four to establish a "poor house" on a county "poor farm." But the problem was ill-defined and solutions always haphazard. Beggars were sometimes auctioned off to farmers or aided by churches or chased from the business district. Hospitals sent bills for paupers to the county courthouse. In 1882 the *Statesman* reported 15 years of public debt for indigent care.

Ada's "farm" for the indigent and feeble-minded began in 1883 with the $5,000 purchase of 160 acres. The property had been subdivided from rangelands homestead by John Hailey, a sheep rancher and stagecoach entrepreneur. Today the closest landmark is the elementary school named for a Boise reformer who campaigned for public welfare, the schoolteacher Cynthia Mann.

Civic associations fed the hope in Ada County and elsewhere that public charity, being a "science," was less expensive than hospital vouchers. Charity, it was assumed, would bridge the social classes, helping the poor become independent. "A little help will put our class of [poor] people in a way to take care of themselves," reported the *Idaho Statesman*. Ada's poor repaid the city by farming and clearing ditches—occasionally turning a profit. But it quickly became apparent that some inmates were too broken for outside labor. Ada commissioners struggled to make clear distinctions between the "able poor" who were healthy enough for labor and the "impotent poor" who were wholly incapable of working the farm. James Murphy of Boise, an "impotent pauper" without family in the Boise Valley, had been sent to the farm at age 71 after breaking an ankle. Another disabled inmate was a gray-headed pauper named Mr. Corder, age 79.

CARTER STUDIO

Bible-toting reformers solicit alms for the poor, about 1896.

Inmates dug ditches to irrigate hay.

In a county that loathed taxation—so hostile to public spending that even the city's drinking water was corporate—club women devised a genteel network of social welfare, raising money through charity balls. In September 1893, at Boise's Natatorium, the Ladies Relief Society raised $333 for poor farm clothing and bedding. The society, said the *Idaho Statesman*, had established "a system of organized charity which is far more effective than any other method."

For county taxpayers the biggest expense was the salary of the farm's superintendent, usually a man who passed the job onto his wife. Eight superintendents live at the poor farm from 1900 to 1912. Paid quarterly, their annual salaries ranged from $600 to $1,000 plus living quarters. Physicians earned about $800 a year to supervise medical care.

Short-term contracts ensured short tenure for superintendents. In 1892, Superintendent Charles Stanton left amid allegations of violent inmate abuse. The county dropped criminal charges after an unnamed female withdrew the complaint. Schoolteacher M. E. Duncan filled the vacant position for $50 a month.

Misfortunate Circumstances

In October 1891, two years before the Warm Springs home for orphans, the *Statesman* reported the tragedy that "six unfortunate children had been thrown upon the county."

The six, called the Jewett children, were discovered in squalor among transients from Iowa and Montana in a muddy shanty near Five Mile Road. Their mother had deserted her husband and run off with her brother-in-law.

Three others sent to the poor farm that same October were the Neal children of North End's Arnold Addition. Elvira Neal, age 3, was discovered with two young siblings, asleep on a soiled couch. Their mother was denounced as "depraved"; their father, a "half-crazed" prisoner in the county jail.

In the women's ward, meanwhile, a young mother named Rose Storms cared for her infant daughter. From Minnesota, Storms had taken the train to Boise to wait for a suitor who never arrived. Storms and the infant joined 23 others at the Ada poor farm. One elderly man was said to have been a protester in Jacob Coxey's "army," a tattered march of the unemployed on the U.S. Capitol Building. Another was Cornelius Sproule of Nampa, who was suspected of being insane.

Abandoned children could be removed to poor farms.

Grand Jury Investigations

Scandal rocked Ada County when an audit uncovered that money had been spent on the poor farm for work than had never been done. At the center was Commissioner J. R. Lusk and $2,000 for road improvements. Lusk, a staunch Democrat, was a plumbing contractor who sold services to the county. His sheep ranch south of the city is now the Lusk District that borders Ann Morrison Park. Elected to the Ada County Commission in 1893, Lusk, it was alleged, had approved some questionable payments. The audit showed a fraudulent pattern of unearned per diems and mileage expenses. Lusk had also tapped poor farm funding for a fine bottle of cognac.

In 1897 the county approved a more vigilant system of audits. Reports showed that the poor farm, selling hay, could sometimes cover expenses. In 1902 the *Statesman* reported that a preacher passing though Boise had praised the farm as a model poorhouse, one of the best in 42 states.

But the mood turned sour in 1912 with a series of damning indictments. A grand jury, convened in September, accused the poor farm of elder abuse. Bedridden inmates left unattended were too weak to reach the outhouse. A blind man in soiled sheets needed immediate hospital care. The physician was "derelict," the superintendent "callous." Jurors claimed that the farm's animals got better treatment than paupers did in Ada County. Antiquated methods of care for sick and senile were "inhumane" and "everything least desired."

Especially abhorrent was a medieval relic in the form of a metal cube to confine the insane. A "living room [for] crazy people," the staff had called it. Standing 9 feet, it resembled a steam boiler. No wall padding inside the cube kept patients from banging their heads.

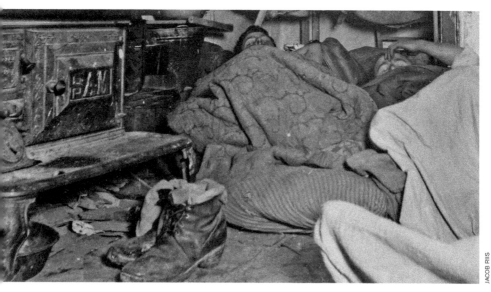

JACOB RIIS

Filth and squalor closed Ada poor farm.

At first the indictment went nowhere. District Judge Carl Davis opined that there was no evidence of malfeasance and it was doubtful that professionals employed by the county had broken the law. The farm's doctor was forced to resign but noted in parting that "a poor farm was not an attractive place under any conditions." It was too much to expect a poor farm to look like a home since, he explained, "the inmates are not from the neat and thrifty class."

But scandal ignited 2 years later on Thanksgiving Day. Good Samaritans who had come to the farm with the traditional holiday turkey found 10 ancient gray-headed men, diseased and crippled. One was said to be 97. The state inspector returned to demand that the farm be condemned. "My recommendation," said J. K. White, "would be to do away entirely with this old, dilapidated, germ-laden bug-infested building." Without cleaning staff, the ward resembled a dungeon. "The system of having these old men take care of their own beds, wash their own clothes and take care of themselves [is] nothing short of criminal." Commissioners were forced to concede that the poor farm concept, a throwback to the 1880s, was hopelessly antiquated. A modern progressive county needed a public hospital with a sanitary nursing home.

Ada County Hospital and Nursing Home, about 1917

Perceptions of Public Welfare

Exchanging one sheep rancher's plot for another, Ada County, in 1916, abandoned John Hailey's pioneer farm above Collister Station for Eugene Looney's 80 acres on Fairview where the trolley turned south at Curtis. The acreage was purchased for 10-fold the price of Hailey's Collister farmstead, about $54,000. No longer known as a farm, the county institution became a respectable two-story building of sandstone with gardens on a manicured lawn. The Ada County Nursing Home, it came to be called.

Today it may seem repugnant that seniors with broken ankles would be left unattended, expected to farm to cover their care. Yet that was not how the program had started. Voluntary and temporary, poor farms had been conceived as humane but also spartan—a means of moral education through virtuous labor, a harsh deterrent for a class of paupers disposed to be indolent. By 1915, however, the nation had changed and so did the poor farm system. The rise of Progressive Era settlement house reformers—Jane Addams of Chicago was one; Boise's Cynthia Mann another—shifted the urban focus to public health and sanitation. Crime, pollution, disease, and overcrowding in 20th-century cities demanded a coordinated and centralized municipal response.

An elementary school at the poor farm's former location honors Boisean Cynthia Mann.

Idaho was ill-equipped for municipal reorganization. Public works elsewhere funded by taxes—drinking water, irrigation, parks, trash collection, electricity, and trolley transit—were privately owned in Boise. Public officials who served on county commissions were often businessmen with a personal stake in competitive enterprises. And so it was in Ada County. Suspicion of government, then as now, fed the distaste for public spending that crippled indigent care.

NAMANNY ASMUSSEN is a junior at Boise State University, majoring in applied science and minoring in history. She was raised in Idaho, competing for the biggest catch with her father and grandfather. After graduation, she intends to pursue a career in the justice system.

Todd Shallat contributed to this chapter.

Hammer and Drill

4

A gold mine recalls the grueling work of dangerous jobs.

by Emily Fritchman

Pearl, Idaho, sits abandoned in the hilly barrens between Emmett and Horseshoe Bend. What was in 1900 a 4-hour trip by horse-drawn wagon is now a 45-minute drive from Boise. West of State Highway 55, the route to Pearl is 5 miles down a dusty washboard road. A heavy rod-iron fence surrounds the first home to appear. Large signs declare, "This Area Is Monitored by Security Cameras." A property-owner nameplate hangs above the entrance to the ranch. Continuing down the gravel road, the entire area is fenced off and marked with "No Trespassing" signs and electric fences. It becomes clear that aside from the gravel road, what used to be the town of Pearl is now privately owned property.

A tiny metal gate surrounds an old mine shaft. The back end of a rusty vehicle juts out from the top of the entrance. Algae-filled water oozes beneath the fence onto the road. The deep run-off ditches were most likely a means of draining the mines. Directly above a cliff-sized mineral deposit, two large, flat pieces of wood jammed into the edge of the hill mark the remains of a collapsed mine shaft.

Willow Creek, the main source of water and gold and the reason for Pearl's earlier existence, has since dried up in certain locations and is overrun with willow trees in other places. As the town of Pearl began to grow and develop during the peak of the gold rush, buildings were erected on both sides of the creek. Whereas in other mining towns abandoned buildings and structures are tourist attractions, the last of Pearl's original buildings were demolished in 2004. All that is left are remnants of old, wooden structures scattered alongside the northern half of Willow Creek. Something that resembles an old piece of bridge leans against the edge of the former waterline, facing the southern half of the creek. It's hard to imagine that this deserted landscape was once a thriving mining town with more than 200 residents, general stores, saloons, boarding houses and hotels, a meat market, and a barber shop.

IDAHO STATE HISTORICAL SOCIETY

With the mines and miners came the businesses to support them.

Mining in Pearl, Idaho

In December 1867, a proprietor of a small stage route in Idaho discovered two veins of gold in Willow Creek, a spot close to Idaho's capital city between the Payette and Boise rivers. Although these findings were relatively minor in comparison to the abundance of minerals in California, this discovery caused a flurry of excitement. "Gold fever" struck both the people of Idaho and those in the easternmost regions of the United States. By the 1890s, additional mineral deposits had been located in this area and capital investment gradually increased. More mines developed and the town of Pearl, Idaho, grew and prospered. Miners removed deposits of lead, zinc, gold, and silver, making the area even more valuable. The Pearl district mines that produced the greatest output include the Checkmate, Lincoln, and Black Pearl mines. In total, the Pearl mines produced nearly a million dollars in profit, much of which came from gold and zinc extraction.

At the peak of activity between 1900 and 1907, the Pearl mines employed about 200 men, 50 of whom were Chinese. The pay rate depended on the position. Whether a timber man, miner, car man, or general laborer, each earned between $3 and $4 a day. According to the 1907 Idaho Mining Industry Report, the average wage for a miner working in Idaho was $3.50 per 8-hour work day, which in 21st-century dollars is approximately $87.58 a day, or between $10 and $11 per hour. Despite the fact that work in the mines was physically demanding, this pay matches that of most contemporary minimum-wage jobs in the United States. Miners worked to support families, labored under miserable environmental

Neil Macaskill tramming ore at the Lincoln Mine

conditions, and received very little financial compensation for the physical and psychological damage sustained under such grueling work conditions.

As exciting an opportunity as mining and the potential for striking gold was for most of these Idaho miners and laborers, the work was difficult, dangerous, and painstaking. Most workers rose early in the morning, around 5 a.m. They spent most of the day with no sunlight, in damp, cramped mining shafts up to 600 feet deep.

The Pearl district mines operated years before technological advances in the 1920s and 1930s made mining safer. Dangerous mining conditions in the early 1900s contributed to a multitude of accidents, sickness, and death among laborers. The frequent use of toxic chemicals for Idaho mining in the early 1900s, including the use of cyanide leaching and nitroglycerine for gold extraction, presented a number of severe health risks, including suffocation, lung disease, and even death. In 1905, approximately 6,000 men were reported as being employed by Idaho mines. Out of these 6,000 employees, at least 20 fatal accidents occurred— an average of 3.33 deaths per 1,000 workers. Men died from the explosion of blasting compounds, rock falls, falling down chutes, contact with trolley wires, collision with a moving cage or car, ground caving, or gasoline tank explosions. These statistics account only for those companies who reported their employment and fatality numbers to the Idaho Mining Industry; it is likely that the death toll was higher, since many men worked for independent prospectors and mining operations.

The frequent application of nitroglycerine blasting compounds that were used for extracting gold contributed to a large number of mining fatalities in the early 20th century. Nitroglycerine compounds used in mining must be heated and cooled at precise temperatures. If handled improperly, the smallest amount of nitro powder can burn and emit significant amounts of carbon monoxide, poisoning miners who inhale it. Over the course of about 30 years in Idaho, the number of mechanical- and chemical-related mining accidents in Idaho claimed the lives of hundreds of working men in the mining

A catalog illustrating mining equipment for processing ore using cyanide

Saloon token, Pearl, 1904

industry, many of whom are lost to history as a result of poor documentation and poor recordkeeping.

One of the many men who lost his life in the mining industry of Pearl, Idaho, was William Albert Ferdinand Kloth. The child of German immigrants, Kloth was born in 1893 in Chicago. As a young adult, he worked as a Western Union telegraph operator until 1910, when he decided to move west and begin a new life for himself in Idaho. In 1915 in Boise, he married Edith M. Franklin, who bore their first child, Virginia Ida, the following year in Pearl.

The streets of Pearl, Idaho, near the Diamond and Checkmate mines

Kloth began working for the mines in Pearl in 1921. His career as a miner was short-lived. According to the *Idaho Statesman*, Kloth was in the process of blasting holes in one of the Pearl mines when he was severely injured by what physicians claimed to be a premature explosion. The blast lacerated Kloth's skin, embedding a rock the size of a fist in his leg and shooting his body full of small rocks. He died 3 days later, on August 17, 1921, at Lewiston Hospital in Emmett. He was 28 years old. The *Idaho Statesman* reported that William Kloth was buried in a Riverside Cemetery in Emmett, Idaho, but his headstone is untraceable.

Decline of a Mining Camp

Over time, the mines in Pearl began to sink as a result of the settling of overlying rock and other material, and the town shrank as economic profits dwindled. By the 1970s, mining operations had completely ceased in Pearl, and the area fell into a state of abandonment. Throughout the 20th century, ownership of the town and the mines contained therein transferred frequently.

In October 2003, the State of Idaho's Department of Environmental Quality submitted a preliminary assessment report to the U.S. Environmental Protection Agency (EPA) investigating possible contamination at the Lincoln Mine site in Pearl. The ore deposits at the Lincoln Mine contained small amounts of sulfide minerals, such as iron pyrite and arsenopyrite, types of fool's gold that contain trace amounts of metal (e.g., arsenic). Over time, these minerals can weather, releasing metals to the environment that can be harmful to people and animals. Because this phenomenon is common among old mining camps in the United States, the EPA regularly investigates these sites and evaluates threats to human health and the environment. By February 2004, the EPA had determined that the risks at the Lincoln Mine site were not high enough to warrant extensive clean-up. This meant that the area did not contain a high enough level of toxicity to be considered a U.S. Superfund site.

The story of Pearl, Idaho, replicates other boom-and-bust mining town stories but is unique in that most of what is left has been destroyed, is privately owned, or is possibly contaminated. The countless "No Trespassing" signs, security cameras, and electric fences prevent the curious from learning about the rich history of this area. What hides below the surface and in the riparian brush of all of this private property may reveal clues critical to understanding this place of hard circumstances.

NCFORESTRANGER

Today a rusted car guards the entrance to an old mine shaft.

EMILY FRITCHMAN is pursuing degrees in history and creative writing at Boise State University. A local history buff, she loves hiking in the Boise foothills. Her favorite American president is Abraham Lincoln.

5 | Razing Levy's Alley

Civic leaders crusaded against prostitution.

by Nicholas Canfield

A kerosene lantern backlit the scarlet curtains above the saloon-bordello called the Bucket of Blood. On June 30, 1892, the *Idaho Statesman* reported that the curtains had closed for "a hard crowd" expecting "a wild orgy." It was a "den of horrors," the *Statesman* continued, where "blear-eyed females" danced with "sodden faced tinhorns . . . whose fond parents no doubt thought they were tucked away in bed." When a "negress" prostitute tossed the lamp at a white customer, the wooden structure barely escaped purification by fire.

Prostitution was a fact of life in frontier cities. In Boise it was barely hidden in the heart of commercial downtown. Wherever men caroused in crowded saloons to drink and gamble, saloon keepers and madams ran prostitution. And wherever rum, fallen angels, and morphine spread vice through the center of cities, crusaders demanded reform.

Prostitution once had its place in frontier society as the "necessary evil" that protected chaste women from dangerous men. Boise's first prostitutes were mostly immigrants or daughters of immigrants. "Cottage" prostitutes worked in hotels and parlors. Often, in city directories, they were listed as seamstresses or housekeepers. More common "crib" prostitutes rented small rooms above saloons or lining the alleys. In Boise by 1890, the crib district extended from about 9th Street to 6th in the alleys bounded by Main and Idaho. Fire insurance maps showed more than 20 saloons with back rooms labeled "FB" for "female boarding." The plumbing was all outside.

The *Statesman* reported "shooting and cutting scrapes and an occasional killing" in the early decades of Idaho statehood. Bawdy saloons included Hart's, Jack Elliott's, and Gilbert's Free Roll, so named for its offer of free chips for playing Faro. Like moths to a flame the district lured "the rough tough men from the mines, the lumber jacks and loggers from the woods, the mule skinners of the freighting outfits, and the ranch hands and riders of the range." Men of higher standing patronized parlors of prostitution in downtown hotels.

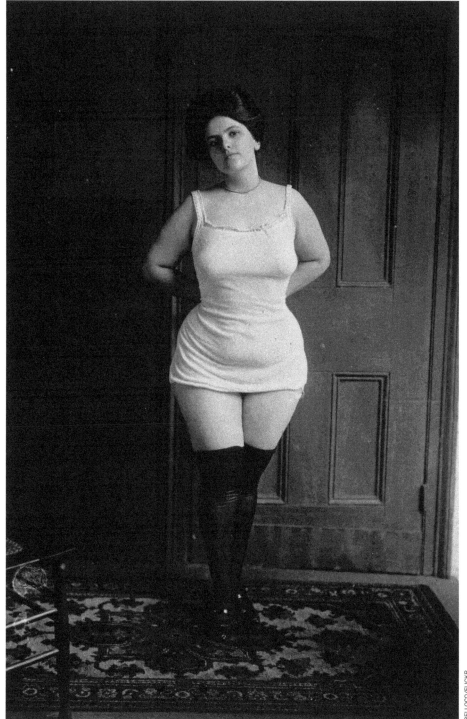

Temperance crusader poster circa 1870

Boise officials mostly tolerated the bawdy houses so long as the vice could be confined. But pastors, boosters, and reformers pushed hard in the other direction. The Woman's Christian Temperance Union, the Columbian Club, the Ladies Auxiliary of the Florence Crittenton Home, and many other civic organizations backed mayors who denounced prostitution, demanding reform.

Davis Levy, the Kingpin

"He is a typical miser – greedy, crafty, and cruel," said the *Idaho Statesman* of the city's most illicit slumlord. Davis Levy came to Boise with the Idaho gold rush. In 1867 he sold cakes and crackers on Main Street near 6th where dance halls and bars still cluster today. Expanding, he opened a grocery store, a saloon, a lunch place, and a candy shop. Sometime in the 1880s—after being assaulted and robbed at gunpoint and after being arrested for "disturbing the peace"—Levy expanded into leasing small rooms for prostitution. By 1893, in the alley behind the 600 block of Main Street, he added 12-foot plank wood cribs. Levy's Alley, Boiseans began to call it.

Municipal government did what it could. On April 1, 1896, the city council ordered the chief of police to cleanse downtown and remove its "fallen creatures." Parlor madams and male proprietors could be arrested or fined.

"Evil in the alleys" became a rallying point for Moses Alexander of Main Street in an anti-prostitution campaign. Alexander, elected mayor in 1900, called Levy's Alley "a menace to public order." It was "monstrous . . . intolerable . . . a disgrace." But police could only charge the miserly Levy with "allowing a house of ill repute to operate in his buildings." A judge found him guilty and fined him $44. Levy appealed, this time going before a jury, who found him not guilty.

Alexander went on to lead the cause for statewide prohibition as the first elected Jewish governor in the United States. Levy, also Jewish, went on to die a deplorable death by strangulation. On April 5, 1901, soon after Alexander took office, Boise police found Levy's rotting corpse in an office above his alley. The body was 3 days cold. Implausibly, the chain of evidence led to another Boisean named Levy (no relation), described as a "whoremonger" and "pimp." The man's name was George "Joe" Levy, said to be a "white slaver" and "Jewish Bohemian" from France. He was captured in Oregon while boarding a ship for Europe. Convicted in Boise, sentenced to hang, commuted to life in prison, he was pardoned for lack of evidence and released. He later returned to the Idaho Penitentiary to serve a sentence for "white slavery." The whoremonger Levy who allegedly murdered the miser Levy of Levy's Alley professed his innocence to the end.

French-Bohemian George "Joe" Levy, convicted of murdering a brothel landlord, 1901

Ellen Bush, the Queen Madam

Ellen Bush was the daughter of Milton Kelly, one of the *Idaho Statesman*'s first owners, editors, and publishers, and Lois Kelly, a prominent woman active in nationwide women's rights organizations. She was also a crib manager. In 1878

LEWIS PUBLISHING

Judge Milton Kelly

Milton Kelly bought 626 and 628 Main Street from Davis Levy. When Kelly died in 1892, he bequeathed the property to his daughter Ellen, who used it for female boarding houses. Bush added at least four cribs to the rear of her Main Street properties, with the alleyway between Main Street and Idaho Street their only access point. Both Ellen and her husband James Bush managed multiple properties designated as "female boarding houses." Ellen took control of the property on Idaho Street when her husband died in 1897. Bush added more cribs to the Idaho Street property around 1898 and managed them all until her death in 1920. As a property manager, Bush leased rooms and spaces on her properties to prostitutes, providing shelter and a relatively safe area for them to practice their trade. One of the people Bush leased space to was Dixie Laurence, who served as a madam for Bush's 620 Main Street property.

IDAHO STATE HISTORICAL SOCIETY

Davis Levy's boarding house, Main Street, 1880

Dixie Laurence struggled in her work as a madam for Ellen Bush. She toiled to improve the 620 Main Street property and went so far as to sublease many of its cribs, while faithfully paying the rent owed to Bush each month. Correspondence between Laurence and Bush's attorney indicated that Bush was pleased with Laurence's work as madam and "'seemed to desire that [she] remain there right along under the same terms and conditions as [she] now had it.'" But in November 1901 Frank Maley, another prominent Boise businessman, "purchased Ellen Bush's interest in the property," thus occluding which property owner owned what land, and how that ownership would affect Laurence and the working girls, who lived and worked with virtually no job, housing, or life security each and every day.

Laurence worked hard to ensure that the women in her employ did not suffer any more than they already did. Madams such as Laurence provided their girls with as many supplies as could be afforded. In return, the girls gave to the madams a percentage of their wages. The madams who worked in Levy's Alley were in essence some of Boise City's first pimps, managing the working girls while simultaneously contending with particular customers and the occasional city official. But despite all of Laurence's efforts, because of the lack of security and options for a better existence, bitter fighting among crib workers was commonplace. Inane acts such as name calling were often responded to with violence—a crib worker stabbing another with a pair of scissors was the most common reply.

In tandem with fighting, depression and suicide were also common experiences. Grace Ashton attempted suicide in September 1903. Grace Ashton attempted suicide in September 1903. She ingested "antiseptic tablets," a common method of suicide among prostitutes. The tablets most likely contained mercuric chloride, with each tablet containing nearly half a gram of the compound. Because they were used for "preventing conception," these antiseptic tablets were commonly found among prostitutes. Acute mercuric chloride poisoning caused protracted and incalculable suffering. The compound acted so quickly that measures such as induced vomiting did not prevent the poison from reaching the stomach. Grace Ashton suffered for nearly a week as her stomach lining dissolved, before she finally succumbed to her injuries. Although she was married and had a living parent, Grace had no family living with her in Boise, and her sister

Mercuric chloride, known as corrosive sublimate in the 1800s, was commonly used as a contraceptive and means of suicide among prostitutes.

workers were her only companions. The women gathered enough money for a funeral service, and Grace was laid to rest in Morris Hill Cemetery. Grace's life and death served as a harrowing example of the type of life lived by the prostitutes of Levy's Alley: almost no protection, no assurances or security, and very little chance of social mobility. Whereas prostitution was a trade in which access and involvement were easy, self-removal and disengagement proved nearly impossible.

IDAHO STATE HISTORICAL SOCIETY

A wagon advertises Moses Alexander's Men's Store on the 700 block of Main Street, about 1896. Alexander spearheaded the anti-prostitution crusade.

Boise's Urban Renewal

It proved hard to obliterate Levy's Alley. Boiseans recall the smell of opium and blue lights, not red, in the 1930s. Skid row bars had semi-clad dancing girls in the 1940s and 1950s, and Boiseans remember prostitution as well. In 1965, the Idaho State Legislature helped Boiseans pave over the menace with legislation allowing for urban renewal. Business leaders hoped to replace the blight with a downtown shopping mall.

At the center of that urban renewal were three city blocks. Spanning Capitol Boulevard, they stretched from Moses Alexander's Men Store to the Turnverein Building in Old Boise, from 9th to 6th along Idaho and Main. The city's police annex, a thrift store, and a row of small office buildings fronted the infamous alley. Properties with brick two-story buildings were appraised at less than $50,000. One disinvested lot was priced

Razing Main Street, 1974

at $0.12 per square foot. Mayor Richard Roy "Dick" Eardley, elected in 1973, thought the alley ideal for a city hall.

In 1975 the bulldozers of urban renewal began flattening Main Street's 600 block for what Eardley called "beautification." Two years later, on Tuesday, March 15, 1975, Mayor Eardley and the Ada County Commissioners officially dedicated the imposing orange-brick Boise City/Ada County building. Boise's new city hall, said the *Statesman*, was "a job well done." The blight had been crushed at last.

Today, appropriately, the city's history office faces Old Boise in the approximate location of the Bucket of Blood. Backlit curtains of scarlet are no longer an embarrassment to the mayor's office or the focus of city planning. City hall's "temperance fountain" is the only oblique reminder of the heyday of Levy's Alley. Erected in 1910 by the Woman's Christian Temperance Union, the fountain recalls the wholesome ideal of the sanitized city that the anti-prostitution crusades hoped Boise would one day become.

WCTU temperance fountain, City Hall Plaza

NICHOLAS CANFIELD is a history student at Boise State University and will graduate in December 2016. His areas of interest include public history, as well as religious and early Christian history.

Colleen Brennan and Todd Shallat contributed to this chapter.

6

Women Behind Bars

Vulnerable women paid poverty's price.

by Ceci Thunes

Poverty is not a crime, yet many people today face criminal punishment for acts that stem from being poor. Municipalities across the country incarcerate citizens for their inability to pay traffic violations or for sleeping in public places, embroiling them in a cycle of debt to the state that jail time will never erase. Even though debtor prisons were banned under an 1833 federal law, people without resources continued to be confronted by the threat of imprisonment.

The women's ward at the old Idaho State Penitentiary was built out of necessity, when women could not reasonably be separated from men in the main facility. The original wooden structure housed the warden and his family, but concrete blocks subsequently encased the structure for security. The male prisoners next door quarried, transported, and cut from the nearby foothills the sandstone that formed the perimeter of the cell house, building an 18-foot high wall that enclosed a space of less than 10,000 square feet.

Barbara Ann Singleton

Completed in 1906, the women's ward housed 214 inmates over the following 61 years. Of those prisoners, a handful were incarcerated twice, mostly for minor offenses, but only one returned more often. Barbara Ann Singleton was 24 years old when she left her small child with family and entered the women's ward at the penitentiary in the summer of 1954. After her fourth sentence ended almost 13 years later, 37-year-old Barbara exited the prison one last time, never to return to those sandstone walls. Her repeated offense was passing checks with insufficient funds.

Similar to many women debtors, Singleton was born without means. She lived in many small towns in Idaho, leaving countless bad checks in her wake. In one of her inmate reports, she claims to not remember all of the places she left those checks, but many found their way back to her, through the criminal courts, and altered the course of her life forever.

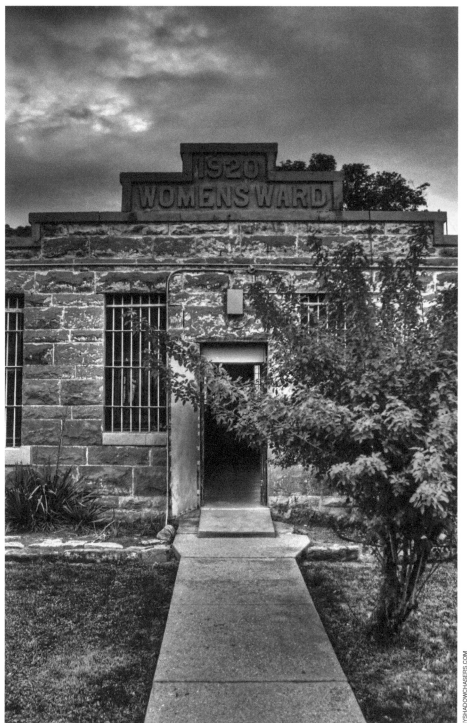

One of her arrests occurred in a grocery store in Twin Falls County, where her parents lived and where she spent much of her non-imprisoned adult life. According to the prosecuting attorney, she "evidently enjoyed writing [bad] checks all over Twin Falls." Two checks totaling $15 (roughly $133 in present-day value) would not normally have landed anyone in the state penitentiary, even in the 1950s and 1960s when incarceration rates for such felonies peaked. But the prosecuting attorney noted that Singleton had passed at least 20 bad checks in the 3 previous years. She had faced prison time and then violated her parole by writing more bad checks.

As the prosecuting attorney told the court, "[Barbara] and her husband . . . just get to drinking and partying and have absolutely no hesitation whatsoever" defrauding local businesses. He added that "several checks" were written to one food and dry goods store alone. But he also believed that

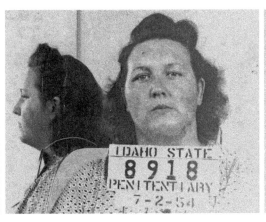

Mugshots of Barbara Singleton

"a lot of Barbara's troubles" were related to her husband, who was also on probation for bad check charges. He expressed a collective concern that the husband was exploiting Barbara by having her bear the legal consequences, not to mention the damage to her status and reputation. The prosecuting attorney also theorized about "the possibility of her having glandular trouble that has affected her rationale." Judge Martin concurred with the attorney's suggestion that Singleton undergo a medical examination and possibly psychiatric treatments, but no evidence of this can be found in her prisoner file.

Barbara Singleton's first imprisonment lasted almost 3 years, during which she experienced a brief parole after a year. She violated her parole within months and was forced to resume her sentence in the concrete cell house. During this time, her father, a World War I veteran, died. Toward the end of Singleton's term, in a document reviewed by the parole board, prison matron Mrs. O'Neil remarked that "lately Barbara has been stirring up trouble," calling her "very deceitful." The prison chaplain offered that "liquor [was a] minor factor" for her, but recommended release, which was granted May 13, 1957.

Freedom lasted 17 months. Barbara wrote more bad checks, totaling $235, left at "grocery stores, service stations, drug stores, and a department store," according to the Twin Falls County prosecuting attorney, Jane Cunningham. Her ultimate conviction rested on a $20 check to Monty's Oil

Women's ward

Company in Hollister, Idaho. The judge imposed a 5-year sentence, but Cunningham had no faith that prison would reform Singleton, believing "if she were released she would do the same thing over again." Her second term was uneventful and relatively brief, about 6 months.

For almost 4 years, Barbara avoided prison. Her clean streak came to a halt just before New Year's Eve 1962. This arrest and conviction indicated that whatever foundation she had was eroding. In her own writing, Singleton admitted she was drunk when, in a Boise Safeway, she attempted to pay with a bad $20 check. The grocery clerk called on funds availability; the check could not clear, so the police apprehended her on the spot. The prosecuting attorney remarked that although Barbara had "no bank account whatsoever," his office possessed 12 other bad checks that she had written in the 8 days prior to her arrest. The *Idaho Statesman* reported that during her trial, Singleton asked Judge Merlin Young for leniency, claiming that she was separated from her husband and had a child at home. Judge Young denied the request, protesting that "her past records as a parolee . . . caused me to sentence her to the penitentiary," adding that she had never been a "fully satisfactory probationer."

Original women's ward building

With the creation of each new inmate file, the story of the transformations in Singleton's life unfolded. Her surname changed, her weight fluctuated, and by her fourth conviction, she had married three times officially and twice by common law. Her one child was the product of her first marriage. Like more than a third of the women incarcerated at the old penitentiary, Singleton listed "housewife" as her occupation.

She never made it past the eighth grade, and no notes indicated a work history that showed promise of making it on her own.

Oral history from Lulu Rowan, the matron of the women's ward from 1961 to 1967, shed light on the more complicated side of this repeat offender. Rowan claimed that one day she came to work, and "Barbara was scared to death." Despite her heft, Singleton was vulnerable. She had been beaten the night before by another inmate, who dragged her out of her bunk and left her "pretty-well battered." The fight was "over something that didn't amount to a hill of beans," according to Rowan. Barbara also managed to escape from the prison once, "but they brought her back," said Rowan.

Inside a typical cell

Rowan quoted Singleton as saying, "I'm what I am. You know what I am." She was more than a poor, sometimes-single mother who wrote bad checks. According to Rowan, Barbara Ann Singleton spent several years in Japan, serving in the Women's Auxiliary Corps as a secretary "for a general or something." Her life in Japan did not set her up well for the future, as Rowan told it, because at some point Barbara fell into prostitution. Rowan claimed that Singleton was also a prostitute for ladies while in Japan, and she "learned how to take care of women, like she was a homosexual, but she was heterosexual." Perhaps Singleton had fantasized aloud about living overseas, or perhaps Lulu Rowan had conflated the stories of her many wards, but no military service was listed on any of the myriad inmate questionnaires and reports processed at all of Barbara's incarcerations.

Rowan got to know her ward intimately, however, and "never had a bit of problem with Barbara, the one who had the twins." At the time of her final incarceration at the old Idaho State Penitentiary, just before Labor Day 1965, presiding Judge Theron W. Ward forwarded his regrets to Warden Louis Clapp: "Sorry to have to send you this pregnant one, but nature will have its way." Rowan, a licensed practical nurse, was with Barbara at St. Luke's Hospital downtown Boise when Barbara gave birth to a girl and a boy. Records indicate that although Barbara was married at the time, a minister and his wife from Oregon met her in the hospital and took the babies away.

For another 14 months after the birth of her twins, Barbara Ann Singleton remained in prison. Her final parole coincided with the year the women's ward closed (1967). All remaining inmates transferred to either California or Oregon. Barbara left the old pen for the last time in spring, with a will to stay sober and a job and husband waiting. While on parole for a year, Singleton found a new life with her family in Nevada, wrote no bad checks, and was recommended for release from parole as a result. It is unknown if that fresh start led to a lasting future, or if she continued to bounce checks and face criminal prosecution, prison, and an ongoing struggle with poverty.

The women's ward in the Singleton era, about 1960

Check Fraud and Bigamy

Over the course of 40 years, many other women with families were confined to the old Idaho State Penitentiary for crimes related to insufficient funds and forgery. Such offenses were not uncommon, and the push to incarcerate gained momentum in the late 1940s. Prosecuting attorneys and business associations cited the increase in check fraud as a growing concern. In an effort to curtail the problem and decrease the burden to the legal system and business community, and with the support of most retail credit associations, the 1949 legislature passed Senate Bill 105, which reclassified insufficient funds checks as a felony and lowered the threshold from $60 to $25.

The policy was a failure. Check fraud did not decrease, and the prison population pushed the walls to its limits. Legislation in 1959 reverted conviction to a misdemeanor status, with some calling for more responsibility to be taken by business owners. They considered it to be a civil matter, much as a contract between two parties is handled, and that police should not be involved. Today, issuing checks with insufficient funds is still punishable by jail time, but the punishment is not as harsh as it was in the 1950s and 1960s.

Other crimes not historically related to poverty can still stem from it. In the late 1800s, aggressive anti–Latter Day Saints sentiment fueled a cultural and political environment that welcomed any legal method to eradicate Mormonism. Politicians and opinion writers of the day had no idea how, generations later, laws regarding bigamy would entangle one "unfortunate girl" in the system.

Daisy Elizabeth Himm

Daisy Elizabeth Himm, the only child to older parents, lost her father to a chronic heart condition when she was 11 years old. Thomas Himm left Daisy and her mother with no means of support. Mrs. Isadora Himm received $18 a month in child welfare from the State of Idaho. "Thank God I got it," Mrs. Himm wrote in a letter to the prison warden Sam Poarch, "for I keep Daisy in school till [sic] she passed the 8th grade." Shortly after she finished school, Daisy Himm married Zeff Parsley in Lewiston, Idaho. She was barely 14 years old. Daisy never lived with Zeff, however, and he "never gave her nothing, not even a pair of stockings," according Mrs. Himm, who maintained guardianship of her daughter.

Despite her mother's care and custody, Daisy ran with a rough crowd. Criminal behavior resulted in her first incarceration, in February 1942, at the Washington

Daisy Himm

State School for Girls in Centralia/Grand Mound. School superintendent Florence Mohahan characterized Daisy's "crime" as an attempted act of extortion aimed at Daisy's uncle, Roy Rickman, who lived in Spokane. In a bizarre retelling of how the 15-year-old staged a game of "vampire" to lure the unsuspecting Rickman into a compromising situation, Mohahan presented a vivid picture of an intentional juvenile delinquent.

Guarding the Idaho penitentiary

In this earliest document found in Daisy's state prison file, another image emerges of a girl who left any tangible notion of childhood long behind. In its absence a young woman with a tough persona is documented in the company of older men, late at night, across state lines, fast on her way to prison or worse, and far from the worried Mrs. Himm of Lewiston, Idaho. "We found her extremely masculine," Mohahan offered, adding that her appearance and behavior were "not a fit subject for this school." She also cited the school psychiatrist's assessment of Daisy, about whom he concluded, "'It is doubtful that her homosexual tendencies can be changed.'" Superintendent Mohahan reasoned Daisy would be better off with her mother and sent her back to Lewiston.

Daisy Parsley returned to the Centralia girls school 4 months later, after committing a crime in California that incarcerated her at the Ventura Reformatory School for Girls, a school that was known for its draconian punishments. So said Mohahan, but a request from the Idaho pardon board to the Ventura school superintendent for background on Daisy provided no record of Daisy's stay there under any of her assumed names.

When Daisy turned 16, she was served divorce papers from Zeff Parsley. Despite the 6-month legal waiting period that began October 14, 1942, Daisy married Paul Hardt 5 days later, in Sandpoint, Idaho. After Hardt left for his army base 9 days later, Daisy joined two young men in an armed robbery in Yakima, an act that sent her back to Centralia. According to Mohahan, "She immediately began to manifest her homosecual [sic] tendencies," created disruptions, and left no room for sympathy in her wake. The superintendent facilitated her next exit after 3 months, reasoning that with the $50 monthly allotment "from her soldier," Daisy shouldn't need to resort to criminal activity for cash. Under supervision of her mother and the Nez Perce County sheriff, Daisy returned to Lewiston on January 29, 1943.

Three days later, she married for a third time. Carl Joseph Van Moulken was a 52-year-old man who had known Daisy "all her life," according to Daisy's mother, who also described him as a "good for nothing fellow." To make her point, Isadora Himm claimed Van Moulken often posed as an FBI agent (with a "15 cent badge, out of the 15 cent store") and threatened Daisy with "harm" and "could cause her trouble" if she did not marry him. Knowing Daisy was already married, Van Moulken had her use a false name, Ramona Lee Dorsey, on the marriage license. The couple was arrested in Lewiston on bigamy charges. Both pled guilty and were sentenced to the state penitentiary for up to 3 years.

3-HUSBAND GIRL' PLEADS GUILTY

Bridegroom, Thrice Her Age, Demands Trial; Will Be Arraigned Today.

Newspapers around the state reported Daisy's legal troubles.

Letters between Nez Perce County prosecuting attorney Marcus Ware, superintendent Mohahan, and state attorney general Bert H. Miller in March 1943 reveal officials did not know how to negotiate the "peculiarities of the defendant girl" and at times seemed determined to punish her harshly. The superintendent wondered what to do with a ward who was "always falling in love with" the other girls, but she advocated that Daisy be sent to prison. She cautioned against sympathy for the minor, as Daisy was "so experienced" and relied on her juvenile status to avoid consequences for her actions.

In his letter to Miller, Ware provided more context for Daisy's circumstances, emphasizing the feedback from the Nez Perce County jail matron and county physician. According to the matron, "there are periods when Daisy manifests female tendencies and shows an interest in sewing, embroidering, etc., and this is followed by a boy-like cycle." The physician labeled her "an hermaphrodite," saying that although "externally she is physically a female, internally she has both male and female characteristics." This vague language was later contested by the state prison doctor, who determined her to be female, specifically noting no evidence of hermaphroditism. This is confirmed in her body report, which also detailed scars from old wounds above the teenager's right eye, on her right shin, and just below her ring finger, on her left hand. On the outside of her left forearm was a tattoo "Grand Mound," whereas inside a tattoo read "T. P. loves S. L."

In his letter to the state attorney general, Ware expressed compassion, noting Daisy's youth, her disadvantaged upbringing, and the fact that Van Moulken was more than just a co-conspirator in their mutual crime of bigamy. He requested recommendation for sentencing on behalf of the trial judge, Miles Johnson, who asked which institution was best equipped to handle Daisy—the state industrial school at St. Anthony or the state penitentiary.

Bert Miller's response was a rambling stream-of-consciousness evaluation. Ultimately he resolved that a sentence at the state school in eastern Idaho would be the most prudent measure to take.

Despite that recommendation—and despite the fact there were no other female inmates currently at the prison and "it would necessitate considerable expense in setting up the machinery for caring for her at the penitentiary"—Judge Miles Johnson committed Daisy to the state prison. He expressed an unreserved lack of faith in her redemption and regarded her as "a menace to society."

Appeals for pardon began immediately. "I am only sixteen years of age," wrote Daisy, on March 25, 1943, "and by all rights should be at home with my Mother." Isadora Himm was 56 years old, alone, and in poor health, which, in part, motivated her persistent campaign for her daughter's release.

In multi-page, hand-written letters to the warden, state pardon board, and the governor, Mrs. Himm asked that "that poor girl of mine" be released immediately. Daisy had been "tricked into this crime" by an older man who "had her afraid." Besides, Mrs. Himm wrote, Daisy "is rightfully married" to an upstanding young man serving in the army during wartime. From Mrs. Himm's perspective, Daisy's imprisonment was a mistake that could be resolved quickly if the authorities understood the circumstances.

The prosecuting attorney recommended that Daisy serve her time in the Idaho State Industrial School Women's Dormitory in St. Anthony, Idaho, versus the state prison.

In her final letter to Warden Poarch, 4 months into Daisy's incarceration, Mrs. Himm's despondency and need for her daughter were acute. She included documentation from a physician to add credibility to her claim that her deteriorating health left her bedridden. She wrote of the victory gardens, the chickens, and the property she could no longer tend to on her own. "It is to her interest she look after it, as it is hers when I am gone," Himm wrote. Mrs. Himm vowed she would look after Daisy, and in return Daisy would help her until the soldier-husband Paul Hardt came home. Isadora Himm sent $3 to the warden as a deposit for Daisy's transportation, so that at the moment of her release, she could travel home.

Mrs. Himm also orchestrated correspondence between Paul Hardt and the warden, Hardt and Marcus Ware, as well as with the governor, C. A. Bottolfsen. By emphasizing Paul's role in providing for Daisy, the broader message was that marriage, not prison, was the most appropriate institution to handle the wayward youth. In Mrs. Himm's mind, her daughter had only one husband—a soldier who willingly offered legitimacy and a hopeful future.

Private Paul Donald Hardt was truly smitten with Daisy, whom he called "Tommy," in a letter sent from a Florida bombing range and addressed to "Mother," Mrs. Isadora Himm. In red pen that ran out of ink as he wrote, Hardt repeatedly expressed his love for, and commitment to, Tommy. "I will come write [sic] down to Lewiston when I get home and see you and Tommy," he assured Daisy's mother. He expressed a sense of duty to secure Daisy's release and understood his role in providing stability for her. "I think I can get Tommy a pardon . . . if she will be good and live with me," he wrote.

Mrs. Himm enclosed a copy of Hardt's letter in her own letter to Governor Bottolfsen. She pointed out that Hardt "is a very good boy" who was coming home on a summer furlough from the military to manage his 160-acre Washington farm. "She would be of great help to him," wrote Mrs. Himm. "As a Broken Hearted mother," she implored the governor to exercise his authority to pardon Daisy, reminding him of her young age and the threat she faced from Van Moulken.

The governor replied the same day his office received her letter. In a brief, indifferent response, Governor Bottolfsen offered no explanation as to why he would not grant her request but assured her he would revisit the matter after the next parole board meeting.

Perhaps Daisy relied on her juvenile status and attempted to manipulate authorities in order to avoid harsh consequences for her behavior. In her first appeal for parole, it is hard to

Woman stands at the prison entrance.

separate sincerity from desperation. "Truly, I am not a bad girl and I am sure there is a lot of good in me," she pleaded, adding, "I sincerely promise that you will not hear evil of me again. I will not leave my mother again."

Daisy Parsley was the only female in the history of the women's ward imprisoned for bigamy. She was also the second, and last, 16-year-old female to serve time there. What distinguished her from Ida Laherty, convicted of stealing horses in 1903, was that Ida was pardoned after 3 months. After 5 months of appeals and negotiation, on her 17th birthday, Daisy was finally given parole and released to her mother.

Ida Laherty

IDAHO STATE HISTORICAL SOCIETY

Within weeks, she returned to the state penitentiary for violating the terms of her parole. Her offense was having stayed out too late with friends. In her appeal to the state board of pardons, Daisy listed the ways in which her behavior had improved: "I'm letting my hair grow, I wear nice little dresses and wouldn't think of putting on a pair of slacks, or being tomboyish," she wrote.

She became a Christian and vowed to listen to her mother, obey her parole conditions, and settle down with Hardt when he returned after the war. This wait lasted 6 months, during which Hardt and the warden agreed to an arrangement in which he would take his young wife out of state to farm and, more important to the pardons board and Warden Poarch, avoid the distractions Lewiston afforded her. On March 1, 1944, Paul D. Hardt left the state penitentiary with Daisy by his side and a personal promise to Poarch "that they would linger in Lewiston only a few days—just long enough for Daisy to visit with her mother."

Daisy was charged with vagrancy in Spokane later that spring. Without the foundation needed to pass less painfully into adulthood, Daisy eventually fell back to a life of crime. A month after reaching the age of majority, Daisy Elizabeth Himm Parsley Hardt faced her first in a string of felony charges that would follow over the years, ensuring the threat of imprisonment became the one constant in her life.

Idaho toilet, Old
Penitentiary Museum

The Cycle of Poverty and Prison

From a modern perspective, it is hard to understand a culture that did not recognize citizens like Barbara Ann Singleton and Daisy Parsley as vulnerable and worthy of protection, even under the conditions of the time. Today one would point to the inefficiency of such righteous measures, not to mention the degrading effect they have on the social fabric. As a collective outlook on what constitutes justice evolves, proper safety nets are placed under those who need it most, but gaps continue to appear. New classifications of crime bedrocked in poverty pull struggling members of society into a continual cycle of imprisonment. For some it may be the inability to afford the penalties of violating traffic laws that create a spiral of servitude to the state. For others the entrenched causes of homelessness turn victims into criminals. Justice is continually redefined by the social and political models of the time. History shows how, in an effort to fit those templates, legislative and judicial action can lead to the unintended consequence of those living outside the margins paying the price.

CECI THUNES has a bachelor's degree in economics with a political science minor from Boise State University. She presented research from this chapter at the 2016 Association for Private Enterprise in Education conference in Las Vegas. She lives in Boise.

God and Reclamation

Farmers waited decades for water.

by Roy Cuellar

"HAVE FAITH IN GOD AND U.S. RECLAMATION" said the prophecy painted on plywood. A famous photograph from 1940 shows the sign standing on double stilts in a barren west of Caldwell. "Desert Ranch," the photo was called (see next page). Government photographer Walter Lubken posed a farm couple next to the sign, their faces stern and determined. The man wears a laborer's cap and canvas coveralls. The woman wears a farm wife's print-cotton dress. Tethered horses flank a Ford Model A amid a scattering of farm equipment. Beyond is the gray desolation of croplands withered by drought on empty canals.

Lubken's "Desert Ranch," widely reprinted, left a portrait that farmers in Canyon County might find hard to fathom today. Sold to the U.S. Bureau of Reclamation, reprinted in government pamphlets, the photograph seemed to suggest hope in the face of hardship. It spoke for a place in time when farmers trusted the government's science, when God was equated with progress and the Feds were His earthly agents. It pictured a West still gripped by the Great Depression yet in the midst of a grand transformation. A parable, an allegory, it framed the distance between independence and the farmer's dependence on projects that flowed federal dollars to drought-stricken lands.

Dashed Expectations

Colorized postcards with nymphs and goddesses sold arid land for the Union Pacific as farmers rushed the Boise Valley on the eve of Arrowrock Dam. A postcard from 1912 showed Miss Ida-ho, the angelic queen of Idaho's harvest. Posed in a fruited crown surrounded by a bounty of Idaho products, she beckoned with natural wonders, with food and fleece and forests and mineral wealth.

Federal dollars for irrigation sustained that promise in Canyon County. On the Boise and Payette rivers—at Lake Lowell in 1908, Diversion in 1909, Arrowrock in 1915, and Black Canyon in 1925—the U.S. Reclamation Service invested more than 400 million inflation-adjusted dollars in one of the world's most remarkable networks of dams and canals. Vast enough to reclaim 300,000 acres, the Boise-Payette Project

watered tens of thousands of homesteads. Its farm economy thrived on soaring demand for wheat and potatoes during the Great War in Europe, 1914 to 1918. But peace in Europe crashed agricultural prices. By 1920, Miss Ida-ho's promise had soured.

Arrowrock Dam, completed in 1915

Depression and drought in Canyon County predated the stock market crash on Wall Street by a hellish decade of dislocation. Arrowrock Dam, an engineering sensation, spilled water though leaky canals with structural failures. Lake Lowell at Deer Flat seeped and silted and clogged with filament algae. Promoters had water for as little as $25 per acre. Farmers paid triple that cost. Congressional investigators in 1924 were shocked to find Idahoans threadbare on shanty farms without plumbing or electricity. Housing on the Boise Project was said to be "far below the ordinarily accepted standards." Everywhere below federal dams were "shacks instead of houses… bareness instead of comforts; cold instead of warmth… mortgages and foreclosures instead of growing bank accounts; sullen hopelessness instead of genial courage." Congress responded. Reinvesting in reclamation, it upgraded the "service" to "bureau" and adopted a more generous fee-based loan repayment system. Five percent of a farm's crop yield became

Sheep ranchers took a double economic hit when per head and wool prices plummeted.

President Franklin D. Roosevelt asks the nation for their continued support for the New Deal.

the most farmers were required to pay to irrigate from federal projects. As commodity markets rose and fell, so did the cost of water.

But the reforms of the 1920s did little to tarnish the myth that prosperity would follow the plow, that new projects in the Boise Valley would eventually cover the cost of construction, that the problem of the Boise Project was too little acreage and too few dams. Bank-financed speculation floated that bombast until suddenly it was too late. In 1932, a year of comeuppance, 1,145 Idahoans lost farms to mortgage foreclosures. Wheat prices dropped to 26 cents per bushel. Sheep dropped to a century low of $2.25 per head. Boise Valley prunes had sold for $22 per ton in harvest before the collapse on Wall Street. In 1932 the prune market crashed from $22 to $6.50 per ton. Sugar beets lost three-fourths of their value, sinking to $4 per ton. Wool prices tumbled from $72 to $18 per ton.

From 1929 to 1932, in aggregate, Idaho's farm revenue fell from $116 million to $41 million. Wages and salaries fell from $139 million to $81 million. Statewide annual per capita income dropped by half, falling from $529 to $268. The blow was violent enough to topple most Republicans from elected office. Governor C. Ben Ross of Parma—elected as a Democrat in 1930, reelected in 1932 and 1934—supported the New Deal of President Franklin D. Roosevelt with its emphasis on western water projects. Canyon County's First Congressional District also went Democratic with Caldwell native Thomas C. Coffin.

The lone Republican from the Boise Valley was Senator William E. Borah. But Borah's colleague in the U.S. Senate was a Democrat as stalwart as any in the era of FDR. Senator James P. Pope of Boise, elected in 1932, became a leader of the Democratic crusade to replace breadlines with work camps. Between 1933 and 1939, Pope and Congress appropriated $300 per Idahoan—a total of $111,804,931. California, by comparison, received $266 per capita. The State of New York received even less. Out of all 48 states, Idaho ranked eighth in per capita expenditures.

Treasury dollars streamed west through dozens of work relief New Deal programs. The Civilian Conservation Corps and the U.S. Bureau of Land Management employed thousands of displaced workers. FDR's Works Progress Administration (WPA) funded more than 500 Idaho projects. Canyon County's WPA served hot lunches, surfaced roads, repaired schools, eradicated weeds, and fought cricket infestations. Canyon County's reclamation funding included $1.6 million to improve dams and canals.

Dry sandy soil made farming impossible.

Grass to Dust

Irrigation, then as now, was mostly snowmelt in Canyon County. For grain, hay, and alfalfa, a year of flood irrigation required 2.5 acre-feet. Vegetables, sugar beets, and potatoes demanded additional late season irrigation. From 1924 to 1938, as farmers added these crops, a water shortage developed. Wind and erosion swept the valley. Idaho storms of drought-stricken soil rivaled the infamous dust bowl that drove the farmers from the Great Plains.

Ditch rider Donald B. Mutch worked for the Reclamation Bureau during years so arid that no water could be released from Lake Lowell. Mutch, in the 1920s, had patrolled canals south of Kuna on horseback. Saddlebags carried padlocks to secure vandalized head gates and a gauge to measure the water

Wind erosion covered the remains of an unsuccessful farm in Idaho.

Farmer tilling dry land

rushing through weirs. Kuna ditches lured snakes, mice, and gophers. One season on the Mora Canal the ditch rider killed 13 rattlers. Water theft was common, but the telephones to report it were scarce. "You had to go to some farm that had a telephone or to the government phone," Mutch remembered. "There was only one on my ride."

Mutch endured some of the driest weather on record. From 1929 to 1934, Canyon County's rainfall was 65% of normal. In 1934, the heaviest rain measured less than a tenth of an inch. Blinding dust suspended air travel. Governor Ross spent Sundays at prayer vigils, pleading for moisture. From late June through the end of August 1934, eight weeks of murderous heat brought no measurable rainfall. At last, on the last Wednesday in August, the *Idaho Statesman* forecasted the hope that a storm might douse the valley. But the storm rained dry sticks and dust. "Governor Ross Drought Relief," the paper derisively called it.

New Dealers responded in 1935 with the founding of the U.S. Conservation Service. Idaho Soil and Water Conservation,

an office in the Idaho Department of Lands, followed in 1939. Depression-era reports show that 27 million Idaho acres had serious erosion problems. In Oneida County, for example, where ranchers ran cattle and sheep near Utah, FDR's Resettlement Administration purchased 140,000 acres to relocate 75 families. Another 9,000 Idaho farmers received loans and conservation assistance via the Farm Security Administration. Historian Leonard Arrington estimated that the New Deal programs sustained Idahoans with $39 million in emergency relief and $50 million in low-interest loans.

Water was hauled 5 miles in oil drums and cans for families enduring the drought.

Desert Ranch

Water, more than the soil, preoccupied Canyon County during the cruelest years of the regional drought. More water meant agrarian votes for New Deal stalwarts such as Senator James P. Pope. On April 24, 1934, the *Statesman* reported success in the senator's negotiations for $1 million for reclamation improvements in Gem and Canyon counties. Pope called the project "a long step toward permanent prosperity."

Senator James P. Pope

On the Snake River Plain and elsewhere lay "millions of acres of unreclaimed land on which nothing of value is produced, but on which abundant crops could be grown."

Among those cheering the loudest were farmers in the sagebrush barrens that came to be called the Black Canyon Irrigation District. Desolate and impoverished, it stretched from the Payette River to the Boise River like a steppe triangle of busted dreams and financial mishaps. Farmers since the

Herbert and Sadie Mersdorf had come to the end of a losing battle against the choking drought when the Resettlement Administration came to their aid with a rehabilitation loan.

1920s had relied on a low concrete dam on the Payette near Emmett. The dam fed canals running south and west toward the farm colonies at Notus and New Plymouth. But the shallow Payette had little storage capacity, and the flow had not been enough to justify regular maintenance. The Bureau of Reclamation responded with pumping stations that lifted water from the Payette River. One beneficiary was Desert Ranch, west of Caldwell. It was there where the Notus Canal crossed the Old Oregon Highway that photographer Walter Lubken found Herbert and Sadie Mersdorf. Posing with the sign proclaiming their faith in God and Reclamation, the Mersdorfs became a cultural symbol. Some said their sign was proof that Idahoans were grateful to Congress. Others said the Mersdorfs were sarcastic and rueful because the flow from the Payette River, long anticipated, had not flowed fast enough.

The story behind the story was that the homesteaders who had cleared the sagebrush were seldom the farmers with the resources to prosper. Land speculators who purchased the farms in foreclosures were the johnny-come-latelies who prospered the most. Herbert James Mersdorf, born in Michigan, had been a Meridian school superintendent before moving to Notus. Sadie hailed from Missouri. Shrewdly, they had waited for Senator Pope and Congress before investing in Canyon County. Faith in God, they well understood, was glorious but not enough to make hay from desert farming; government was essential as well.

ROY CUELLAR is a retired pilot and the father of three daughters, all graduates of Boise State University. He graduated from Boise State University with a bachelor's degree in applied science with a minor in history and a concentration in geosciences.

Todd Shallat contributed to this chapter.

Gallery: *Out of the Dust*

by Todd Shallat

New Dealers sold resettlement programs with conservation morality tales. From 1933 to 1941, when great storms of swirling dust chased farmers from Snake River farmsteads, photographers documented the devastation, cheering government aid.

Three of Idaho's most talented storytellers were Arthur Rothstein, Dorothea Lange, and Russell Lee, all photographers with FDR's Farm Security Administration. Rothstein of New York first reached the Boise Valley in May 1936. Lange of New Jersey tracked migrant farm hands. Lee of Illinois studied Canyon County as the farming rebounded with water from the Payette River in 1940 and 1941. Thousands of memorable photos—of jalopies Idaho-bound on the Old Oregon Highway, of high school stoop labor in pea fields, of farmers on resettlement projects, their families living in tents—show gumption in the face of hardship, triumph in times of despair.

But few of the Idaho photos were published. Preserved on microfilm, they remained negatives never developed and mostly unknown until the age of digitization. Our Idaho sampling features the fate of farmers on New Deal resettlement projects. We begin with the epicenter of dust in southeast Idaho's Oneida County. The rest show labor and living conditions of the Okie migration to Ada and Canyon counties. All are in the public domain in the Library of Congress's collection from the Farm Security Administration and Office of War Information, 1936-1943.

One of the families resettled from exhausted land in Oneida County, Idaho. By Arthur Rothstein, May 1936.

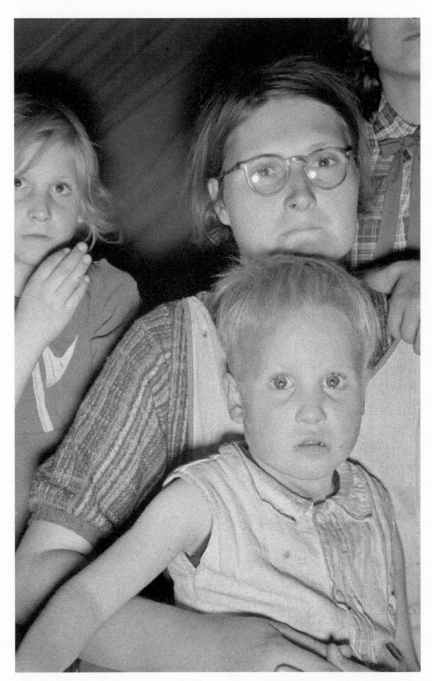

Family of six in tent after supper. Came to potato harvest after father was laid off of WPA in Boise, Idaho. Oldest child is 12. Little boy has dysentery. By Dorothea Lange, October 1939.

Chuck wagon in which part of family of 14 lived. Oneida County, Idaho. By Arthur Rothstein, May 1936.

Migrants bound for an Idaho resettlement camp. By Arthur Rothstein, July 1936.

Pile of bleached bones of horses and cattle that have died on the overgrazed land in a resettlement development area, Idaho. By Arthur Rothstein, May 1936.

Bagging wheat on an Idaho farm cooperative. By Russell Lee, July 1940.

Laborers bring in hampers of peas, Nampa, Idaho. By Russell Lee, June 1941.

Farm workers unloading their car and moving into tent in which they will live at Wilder's migratory labor camp mobile unit. By Russell Lee, May 1941.

Dust bowl migrants. Left Texas to work the cotton and fruit harvests, reaching Idaho via California and Oregon. By Dorothea Lange, September 1941.

Widow husking corn on the Black Canyon Project in Canyon County, Idaho. By Russell Lee, November 1941.

Filling station and store across the street from a labor camp, Caldwell, Idaho. By Russell Lee, June 1941.

High school girls waiting go work in the pea fields, Nampa, Idaho. By Russell Lee, June 1941.

Children in school at farm workers' camp in Caldwell, Idaho. By Russell Lee, May 1941.

Laborer with hamper of peas, Nampa, Idaho. By Russell Lee, June 1941.

When you deliver a hamper of peas to the checker he gives you this check redeemable once a week. Nampa, Idaho. By Russell Lee, June 1941.

Widow husking corn on the Black Canyon Project in Canyon County, Idaho. By Russell Lee, November 1941.

Farmer, Canyon County. By Russell Lee, June 1941.

8 | Nazis on the Homefront

Boise Valley farmers enlisted prisoners of war.

by Susan Hook

By December 11, 1941, when the United States entered World War II, tens of thousands of German and Italian soldiers had already been captured in combat. America rushed in to relieve the overcrowding. Troop ships returned from Britain with more than 400,000 enemy combatants. Hundreds of prison compounds and camps sent inmates into the agricultural fields during a time of extreme labor shortage. Prison labor was especially welcome in the Boise Valley. Boise Valley crops—especially the sugar used to make explosives—had become vital munitions of war.

Base camps, 175 of them, popped up across the United States, in every state except Vermont, Nevada, and North Dakota. Smaller branch camps, 511 of them, reported to these main camps. It was more efficient to house the prisoners closer to the farms that needed the labor.

In the Northwest, the U.S. Army built Camp Rupert near Paul, Idaho, to oversee a network of 23 small branch camps in Idaho, Utah, and Montana that eventually held 15,000 Italian and German prisoners of war (POWs). Base Camp Rupert resembled a small city, with its 172 buildings, including barracks, mess halls, a hospital, and a church. Workers built smaller Idaho branch camps in Aberdeen, Blackfoot, Emmett, Filer, Franklin, Gooding, Idaho Falls, Marsing, Nampa, Payette, Pocatello, Preston, Rigby, Shelley, Sugar City, Thomas, Upper Deer Flat, and Wilder. Considered "temporary" camps that would be closed during the winter, the branch camps consisted mostly of tents. Groups of farmers and sugar companies built many of them.

The Upper Deer Flat Labor Association constructed the Upper Deer Flat Branch Camp on the Swartz farm south of Nampa and began housing prisoners in May 1945. Tents were used as barracks. Each of the six-man tents held seven prisoners. The overcrowding was explained away to the Red Cross inspector by the "temporary" placement of an additional 50 prisoners at the camp. A 220 × 330 foot barbed-wire fence enclosed the camp. Inside this restricted area stood a kitchen/mess hall (150 × 20 ft.), bathhouse (20 × 50 ft.), and pit latrine (20 × 30 ft.). Well water was supplied by the Upper Deer Flat Labor Association. Open ditches drained into an irrigation canal.

time, I was on my way to Africa and after a stop in Naples, we finally joined the Africa Korps. On May 1943, the war in Africa was over, and after weeks of misery Americans took over and shipped most of us to the U.S.A. We landed in Norfolk, Va. and soon found ourselves in a POW camp in Tonkawa, Oklahoma. I spent three years, mostly in the west, in different locations (Texas, Arizona, New Mexico, Oregon, Washington and Idaho). I was, may b

13.5.43 GEFANGENNAHME

5. 6. " TUNIS

13. 6. " SOUKH EL CEMIS

14. 6. " BONE
3. 8. " ABF. N. U.S.A.
27. 8. " ANK. " "

30. 8. " TONKAWA (OKLA.)

27. 5. 44 HASKELL "

McALESTER "
WETUMKA "
3. GRU R "

17. LOR (K.M.)
30. 5 } ELOY (ARIZ.)
9. 5. " }

12. 6. 45 } Ft. LEWIS (WASH.)
20. 6. " }

20. 6. " ADAIR (ORE.)
20. 4. 46 NYSSA (")

US troops train for the campaign in Africa.

e than 150,000 POWs ived in the US after surrender of General n Rommel's Africa Korps.

©BRIGITTE CARNOCHAN 2008

The Franklin Farm Labor Association built a second branch camp in Nampa, located on Franklin Boulevard about a half mile north of Ustick on the east side of the road. The army described it as "5 miles north of the town of Nampa in the heart of the Snake River Irrigation District." Accepting prisoners beginning in May 1945, this camp consisted of 45 six-man tents housing 260 prisoners in a fenced area 337 × 280 feet. A single-strand barbed wire with an overhang encircled the camp.

Local farmers built the Emmett Branch Camp to hold a few hundred POWs. Farmer Wayne Harper noted that it was constructed on Main Street in Emmett.

As a nod to the labor unions, applicant farmers submitted paperwork detailing their need to use the prisoners for labor and stating that no other labor was available. The War Department required farmers to pay the same rate they would have paid civilian laborers had they been available. This rate was "the difference between the prisoners' 80 cents (paid by the government), and the standard daily wage after deducting the employers' cost of transportation, housing, and security."

The money went directly to the U.S. Treasury and became a source of profit for the U.S. government. Months before the end of the farm labor program and the repatriation of the POWs, Lieutenant General Blackshear M. Bryan, the head of the War Department Prisoner of War Division, announced to Congress that as of June 1945, the government had profited by $22 million.

General Blackshear Bryan commanded the U.S. Army's Prisoner of War Division.

The Upper Deer Flat and Franklin Labor Associations contracted with the government for 10,125 man-days of POW labor between May 10 and June 30, 1945, for the following work:

Beets – thinning	$10 seg – $12 reg	.4–.5 acre
Beets – hoeing	1st $4 – 2nd $2.50	1.25 acre
Onions – weeding	$25–$15–$10	.2–.3–.5
Lettuce – thinning	$10 acre	.5 acre
Potatoes – veg seed hoeing	60 cents/hour	
Cleaning irrigation ditches	60 cents/hour	

Few of the guards spoke German, so prisoners received handouts in German and English with instructions on how to work the crops. Amalgamated Sugar also produced a training film.

Even tiny Fruitland had a small temporary POW camp that held no more than two dozen POWs in a corner of the city park. In an oral history recorded for the Idaho Historical Society in 1995, farmer Albert Naher of Fruitland remembered his first encounter with the prisoners who were there to help him thin his apples. "We got the ladders June the 29th so they—Yeah. They came June the 30th, 24 in a truck with a guard." The guard told Naher, "They're from the Africa Corps, the North Africa Corps. These guys are tough. They're rough." The guard instructed Naher not to give them anything. "Just do your business," the guard said. "Tell them what to do and not what to do . . . and just kind of stay away." A German sergeant accompanied the prisoners. It was the sergeant rather than the guard (who didn't speak German) who controlled the prisoners. "The Sergeant barked out an order and they fell into formation," Naher said. "They didn't walk down the orchard. They fell into a formation, and they marched."

Guard keeps watch as prisoner works in the field.

Infantryman of the Africa Corps with sand goggles and a dust cloth over his face.

During wartime, women helped with the harvest.

Because Naher spoke German from childhood, he had friendly conversations with the prisoners, even though the rules forbade it. Asked if his opinion of the prisoners changed after word got out about the concentration camps, Naher replied, "The people in this country, the ones I know, they didn't really hate the Germans as such. They hated Hitler and his regime." After the war, Naher's church sponsored some refugees. Naher asked one of the refugees, Fritz Johnson, why, if he saw the concentration camps, he didn't do something. Fritz replied, "If you complained, you wound up in there."

Emmett farmer Wayne Harper explained that the labor shortage occurred because so many men in the community were off fighting in the war. "During the cherry harvest," he said, "I harvested two or three years with nothing but 14-year-old to 18-year-old girls. These girls were brought over from Boise. . . . They were instructed [to] come over here and do war work. In other words, harvest the fruit. The kids found out they could make some money so they worked." Harper insisted the German POWs worked hard. "Of course, they were good help," he said, "because if they didn't fulfill their quota, they slept outside in September, and were stripped without anything but a pair of shorts on. So they had to work." Harper claimed the army enforced the rules and set the quotas. "Every man had to pick 17 boxes [of prunes]. That's 850 pounds, which doesn't sound like it's an awful lot, but the orchard was old and hard to pick."

The Geneva Convention established rules for treating prisoners humanely in the areas of housing, food, clothing, medical attention, hygiene, and even education. The War Department insisted that these rules be followed in order to protect U.S. soldiers held captive in Europe. Branch camps did not always enforce the rules. Some of the camp commanders added rules of their own. The Franklin Labor Association distributed the following rules to its members:

Supervision – Details going out for the first time must be given proper instructions on how to best work the crop so as to accomplish maximum production. The farmer or his representative must be in the field at all times.

This was the last picture. 1942

©BRIGITTE CARNOCHAN 2008

Transportation – No prisoner will be loaded in a car or truck unless there is a seat where he can sit down. No trailers will be used which do not have brakes.

No person will be allowed to talk to the prisoners except the guard and the farmer or supervisor in charge of the work.

No women or children will be associated with the prisoners of war in any category.

Artist Brigitte Carnochan created photo memories of her father, a German soldier in Erwin Rommel's elite Africa Corps, who was captured when she was just 18 months old. He served time in Camp Rupert located near Paul, Idaho.

An army inspection report dated August 30, 1945, described the poor living conditions at the Franklin Branch Camp. Prisoners lived without electricity or hot water. "Here, as in a number of the Rupert branch camps," the report said, "electric wires run to the compound fence but do not enter. The camp commander believed that candles were on the way, but was not sure. No hot water for bathing and washing purposes is provided. Agricultural workers, who leave the camp at 6 a.m., do not return until 7 p.m. or later." In effect, the prisoners were never in their tents during daylight except for their one day off each week.

The report also documented the lack of other amenities. "The Canteen system is deplorable, not only due to lack of organization but also due to the scarcity of money among the prisoners." Although prisoners were supposed to be paid 80 cents per day for their labor in canteen scrip, receipt was often delayed for weeks or months due to government red tape. Unless the prisoner could arrange credit, he could not buy soap, tobacco, needles, writing paper, or personal items that were not provided by the camp.

Canteen scrip was issued in denominations of 1, 5, 10, and 25 cents.

The same inspector reported very low morale at the Upper Deer Flat camp: "Eighteen recently refused to work, but after five days confinement and restricted diet they decided to resume labor." Restricted diet meant bread and water only. Prisoners' punishment was a maximum of 30 days in prison, maximum 2 weeks on bread and water. (No prisoner at the Franklin or Upper Deer Flat camps had ever been given the maximum penalty.) The report points out that guards were returned American veterans who, having seen the atrocities committed by Nazis in Europe, antagonized the entire group of prisoners under their supervision. The camp commander, Captain Michael Woronovich, also treated the prisoners poorly. He provided no recreational opportunities for the men and no electricity or candles despite saying he had requisitioned them many times. The 50 "temporary" prisoners lacked adequate shoes, blankets, and clothing. Administrators at Base Camp Rupert refused a requisition of mattresses for these men because the shipment would require a boxcar and cost $830.

By the fall of 1945, resentment was growing among the POWs, who had expected to go home once the war was over. Germany had surrendered in May, and the Geneva Convention required repatriation. According to a *Statesman* article, lack of railway transportation caused delays in repatriation. POWs in Idaho would work until November 24, even though the contract with the labor association had expired.

The logistics of getting nearly 400,000 prisoners home, plus the scarcity of available farm laborers nationwide, caused some constituents to put pressure on Congress to not only keep the POWs in the country but also to import more prisoners being held in Europe. This never happened, however.

The last POWs left the Idaho branch camps on July 10, 1946, according to a *Statesman* article published July 11. The article bemoaned their departure: "The farm labor situation

U.S. FARM SECURITY ADMINISTRATION

Harvesting beets

worsened as approximately 620 German prisoners of war left the Upper Deer Flat, Franklin, and Wilder camps for parts unknown."

Treaties with some countries required that POWs be returned to France, Great Britain, and the USSR to help with reconstruction. It was 4 years before some of the prisoners that were sent to work in France and Britain could go home. One group of German POWs scheduled to be returned to the USSR was killed on the dock by the crew of the Soviet ship that was scheduled to pick them up, and the USSR kept some prisoners in forced labor for up to 10 years.

A dilapidated building is all that remains of a POW labor camp in Nyssa, Oregon.

By 1947, Camp Rupert ceased to exist. Anything that wasn't sold at auction was hauled off. The original tents and single-strand barbed wire, the latrines and mess halls are gone now. This may explain why most Idahoans don't know the camps even existed. Almost no structures remain to show where German POWs lived and worked as field hands. There's nothing to see but empty farmland and a few small subdivisions where the Franklin Branch Camp used to be. B&E Storage Rentals now occupies the site of the old Emmett Branch Camp. One of the Upper Deer Flat guard towers that survived for more than 60 years on the Swartz farm south of Nampa blew down in 2006, after being moved closer to the farmhouse and used as a playhouse for generations of Swartz children. Descendants of the same family still grow sugar beets on the farm. A small wooden structure still standing on the farm belonged to the camp, and the crumbling cement pads that sat under the prisoners' tents are now used to keep farm equipment out of the mud.

Bodies of the six German soldiers that died while captive in Idaho were initially buried at Camp Rupert, then transferred later to the Golden Gate National Cemetery in San Bruno, CA. The U.S. government offered to ship their bodies back to Germany if their families paid for it, but none could manage the expense. In the end, no prisoners who died in Idaho ever made it back to Germany.

WWII had brought the unexpected. War had brought air bases, industry, high prices, rationing, and, in Idaho, an urgent shortage of farm hands. War prisoners joined Mexicans, Japanese Americans, and local teenagers in the multicultural mobilization needed to harvest the crops. There were those who thought the prisoners pampered. Others felt ethnic kinship. In a valley where German was widely spoken and where one in five Idahoans claimed to be ethnically German, it was possible to detach the Nazi horrors from misfortune of common soldiers in global events beyond their control.

SUSAN HOOK retired from the communications industry in 2010. She graduated from Boise State University in 2015 with a degree in multidisciplinary studies and a certificate in dispute resolution.

South of the Tracks

Housing segregation isolated the marginalized.

by Pam Demo

The streets of Ash, Lee, old Lovers Lane/Pioneer Street/Pioneer Walkway comprise more than a century-old distinctive street grid within its larger River Street neighborhood. The streets drew culturally diverse working-class neighbors struggling to make ends meet. The now tattered and disintegrating setting and its unique cultural history was home to immigrants, people of color, and those who the city's other neighborhoods could not or would not accommodate.

River Street, south of the tracks, Colored Town, river rats were collective terms imposing Otherness on residents who lived along the streets in the former railroad district south of Grove and north of the Boise River. The city north of the now-missing tracks stigmatized and segregated the neighborhood lying between the Boise River and the railroad district. When the Outside cared to take notice, its take on the neighborhood was skewed.

After 1893, when the Oregon Short Line reached Tenth Street Station, oil tanks and warehouses bordered the railroad district. Developers filed densely platted additions that filled vacant land. By 1912, small wooden houses lined Lee Street, Ash Street, and Lovers Lane. Several were unique in style and few remain standing today.

Permanent residency was an exception. A single wage-earner supported a household, and blue-collar employment or no employment was the norm. Extended families and boarders commonly lived at a single address. With few exceptions, residents were working-class, at home in the neighborhood until they could afford to leave.

Stigmas and Stereotypes

Juanita Aberasturi Iribar clearly recalled "across the tracks" stigma that came with growing up Basque on Ash Street in the 1920s and 1930s. For Juanita, stigma was clear in the epithets "river rat," "poor white trash," and "black Basco."

DARWIN OSWALD/IDAHO STATESMAN

Lovers Lane on Pioneer Street epitomized the Otherness that white Boiseans stigmatized. "Pioneer Street was a street, a block maybe," Cherie Buckner-Webb remembers. She lived on the street as a toddler in the 1950s until her family broke the color barrier with a move to Boise's North End. "There were shanties when I was growing up," said Buckner. "Maybe only two, three or four of them were functioning maybe as juke-

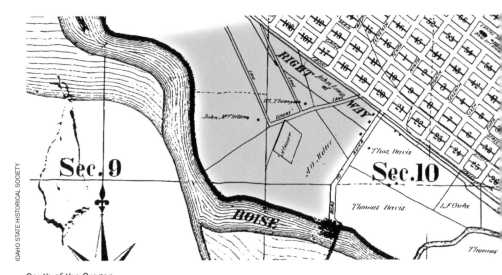

IDAHO STATE HISTORICAL SOCIETY

South of the Oregon Short Line, about 1900

Previous page: Erma Madry Hayman at 617 Ash Street

joints, but they weren't even enough together to be juke-joints."

Still, the street with its district called Lovers Lane had a bawdy reputation for gambling, bootlegging, and prostitution. Black soldiers stationed at Mountain Home and Boise's Gowen Field were welcomed. Boise police left the district alone. Carousing was ignored "as long as you kept it off Main Street," said Buckner-Webb.

But Doris Thomas of Lee Street felt no need to lock her doors. Recalling the 1950s, she remembers a vibrant mix of black and white and immigrant neighbors. All found ways to make a living. When circumstances changed, they found reasons to move on.

In the 1950s and 1960s, few residents owned their homes. South of the tracks was mostly rentals. Safe and neighborly, it was a tight-knit enclave of Basques, African Americans, European immigrants, Chinese, Hawaiians, and resident working-class whites.

Working Mother of Six

Doris Thomas lived in the Lee Street neighborhood for 60 years. As a mother of six and lifelong restaurant worker, she loved the mix of neighbors and the endless opportunities for kids growing up down by the river, south of the tracks. Vacant lots abounded, nearby ballpark events were free entertainment, kids skated at the Riverside Dance Hall, and everyone learned to swim in the river. When the circus came to town, it set up a block away. Families listened to the radio, walked uptown to the public library, sat on their porches to visit, went to the ballpark for games, and played cards. Most had no cars and little money but made the most of what entertainment they could easily and cheaply create themselves.

Doris came from Missouri to Boise in 1926. She first lived on Ash, then moved to Lee. She and her husband Jack worked in the restaurants, coffee shops, and bars while raising five sons and a daughter. When Jack died at age 61, he was still employed in a restaurant uptown. Years later, in 1980, Doris retired at 1114 Lee, her hands crippled by years of waitressing.

Doris's perception of her neighbors' commonalities and differences was expressed in terms of those belonging to the neighborhood as being "residents of Idaho" or "residents of the neighborhood." For her and others, longtime residency outweighed ethnicity in determining who was different; time living in the neighborhood trumped skin color. Her neighbors "weren't the ones that came from the outside," she explained. Those from the outside were different. "They're the ones you had the trouble with."

Known as "Mrs. Jack," Doris walked home on 11th and Pioneer streets from her late-night work shifts at The Grill, The Casino, and other eateries. She respected her Lee, Ash, and Pioneer neighbors and in return she felt at ease walking to work late at night on dark streets south of the tracks.

Following Prohibition, the Thomases lived at 1119 Lee for almost 13 years. Doris claimed that the previous "Austrian" residents at 1119 were bootleggers. The men had rigged the window sills with springs that, when triggered, revealed hidden storage for liquor. Her years of working

Bernease Rice and her son, Lee Rice, II, near River Street, about 1950

Boise's restaurants, especially the night shifts, meant that Doris Thomas was familiar with the city's cast of characters who bootlegged during Prohibition, ran gambling establishments, and ran women. Clearly it all happened as readily uptown as it did down by the river. Uptown racial discrimination was more perplexing, distressing, and corrupt in Doris's eyes than was gambling, boozing, or running women in the Main Street hotels and side-street rooming houses. Blacks were not allowed to be served, she was told by her bosses.

She noted that during the war, visiting black servicemen received the same restaurant and bar discrimination as did Boise's black citizens: they might order at the counter or bar but they certainly had to drink and eat out on the curb. White patrons shunned eateries and staff that readily served African Americans. The waitress from down-by-the-river was piqued by uptown racial distinction and disrespect. For Doris, prejudice on the city streets surprised her. "It doesn't seem to me like the prejudice would be that bad, but it was," she said.

In 1965, Doris Thomas was widowed and living in an elegant red-brick house at 1114 Lee. For a lifetime she was proud of her working-class history, her neighborhood, and the ties that bound neighbors of all colors and cultures together. "It was a nice area . . . a grand area."

Blacks and Basques

Robert Gilmore, a black Boisean who lived on Lee Street, was active in Boise's 1907 Colored Progressive Club. Gilmore worked as a porter for W. M. Sharps in 1910 while supporting his wife and five children. Between 1912 and 1913, the Gilmores and three children were living on Grand, not more than four blocks from Lee.

In 1910, the black Thorpe family and Elijah Glass, a black miner, were neighbors on Lovers Lane. The Mayos and Wilsons residing on Ash, the Mayfields and their neighbors on Miller, and the Gilmores on Lee were families of color, designated in the U.S. Census as "Mu" (Mulatto) or "B" (Black).

By 1920, according to the Black History Museum archives, 63 blacks lived in Boise. Alex Simons, a barber, lived on Ash. In the 1930s, Marie Maynard resided at 1118 Miller next door to the Buckner/Lawrence family, and a black family lived at 1114 Lee Street.

Black residents lived at 1114 Lee from 1961 to 1963. A River Street relative recalled visiting them at the elegant brick house in the early 1960s. Thereafter, until the late 1970s the River Street area was home to many in Boise's black community. Pioneer, Ash, Miller, River, and Grand, South 13th, 14th, and 15th, and Lee continued to define 70 years of the community's "place" in the city.

IDAHO STATE HISTORICAL SOCIETY

Warner Terrell, Jr., of South 14th Street, 1920

Boise's Basques mostly clustered near the Grove Street boarding houses. By 1903, some lived on the north end of Ash Street as well. The first residents were single men, mostly sheepherders who wintered in Boise. By 1915, entire families lived on Lovers Lane and its intersection with Ash. Families and individuals had moved onto Lee by 1917, remaining next door and down the alley from their extended families and friends at the intersection of Ash and Lovers Lane until the 1950s. While the men left town to work on the ranches, the women and children remained at home. Cousins, nieces,

Basque immigrants,
Boise, 1911

siblings, mothers, and grandmothers gathered into single-family dwellings next door or down the alley at the Lee/Ash/Lovers Lane intersection.

In 1912, one of Boise's first Basque *frontons* (handball courts) was in use on Lovers Lane at the intersection of two alleys, a block north of the original River Street alignment. Henry Alegria recorded in his memoir that in 1910 Jose Eguren lent $1,000 to Domingo Zabala to build the two-walled fronton at 631½ Lovers Lane. Zabala resided next door to the fronton, then moved to Nampa in 1915, leaving it to Manuel Aberasturi. Marselino and Marie Arana briefly operated a bakery in it in 1916.

More than a dozen Basque families lived in the neighborhood between 1930 and 1952. Doris Thomas knew them all but found it hard to talk to the older ones because they were "old country" and spoke only Basque, whereas their children spoke Basque but also learned English.

Juanita Aberasturi Iribar entered first grade speaking only a few words of English. Her brother Juan spoke none. Speaking only Basque, both children picked up English "on the streets" and as best they could in school. Their family lived on Ash from 1917 until 1935. The women often visited on a bench outside the Aberasturi's barn while the men were away for much of the year. "Basques are very clannish," Aberasturi Iribar observed in a 2005 interview. The next-door houses at 1118 and 1120 Lee were long and close together so the women could visit through the open windows.

By the 1930s, many Basques turned to businesses other than herding as they settled in the Boise Valley. In 1952, Ignacio Alegria's family was the last of the Basques to move from the neighborhood, closing a chapter on 50 years of immigrant *Euzkaldunak* and *Amerikanuak* Basque presence in the Ash/Lee neighborhood.

By the 1939s the ethnic mix also included Hawaiians, Greeks, and Slavic Eastern Europeans. Bohemian Czech-Slovak immigrants rented on South 14th Street, and a Japanese family lived nearby.

Housing Was Humble

Lathrop-Matevia house at 1114 Lee Street, lost to urban renewal

The red-brick house at 1114 Lee was an elegant and unique face in the neighborhood with its gables, steeply sloped roofs, decorative shingles, ornate front porch, and iron fence. In 1905, machinist Frank Lathrop was its first resident. Subsequent history reflects long- and short-term residencies of several to at least seven people, including railroad and freight-yard workers. Restaurant owners William and Emma Matevia were owner-residents from 1925 to 1943, taking in occasional boarders. The Matevias installed the neighborhood's first phone, which anyone could use, day or night.

According to the U.S. Census Bureau, in 1930 the Matevias' house was worth $3,000, one of the highest values in the neighborhood. The house at 633 Ash, which later became the Thomas family home for years, was valued at $3,500.

Matevia owned the popular Pure Food Café on Main Street between North 10th and 11th streets. Jack Thomas worked as a cook at Matevias' café, and for years the family rented 1119 Lee from the Matevias. By 1944, Matevia had moved across the street from 1114 Lee to 1119 Lee, the house he formerly rented to the Thomases.

Maude Bailey was another long-term resident at 1114 Lee. In 1950 she remodeled the front porch, and 6 years later

Erma Madry (Hayman) at the piano with the family's band, about 1915

she built the red-brick garage on the alley. Into the early 1960s, 1114 remained a well-kept, distinctive residence with its expanse of gleaming hardwood floors, oak woodwork, and unusual bay windows. Four years after Jack's death, Doris moved into 1114 and occupied it until her death in 1986, lamenting her inability to keep it up.

A history of house photos captures the decline and fall of once-handsome 1114 Lee Street. In 2006, the faded face was leveled and replaced by a dirt parking lot. The rise, decline, and fall of 1114 Lee reflect the rise, decline, and fall of its neighborhood.

Doris Thomas saw how things had changed over the 60 years she had spent on Ash and Lee: "I think they really call it a slum area now from what they used to," she noted in 1980. As an elderly white woman among white and black neighbors, her view of neighborhood decline was not related to safety but to failure of landlords to maintain property and choose tenants carefully.

In a 1980 interview, Dorothy Buckner put the issues of substandard housing and landlord-tenant relations squarely on the shoulders of the few white landlords who had long owned most of her Pioneer Street neighborhood. Buckner's daughter, Cherie, explained her family's incentive to leave their black neighborhood in spite of the difficulties they would face trying to move into white neighborhoods north of the tracks. She recalled that along Pioneer, "housing was humble" and that there was stigma associated with being from south of the tracks.

Although the Buckner women spoke of pride for their neighborhood, by 1957 they could afford to live elsewhere and get out from under the thumb of landlords. The family moved to the North End and stayed there in spite of what Buckner-Webb described as a "first-class cross burning" on their front lawn after they had moved in.

Erma Hayman lived in her well-kept house on Ash for more than 50 years. In a 1980 interview she stated that the ethnically mixed neighborhood was the only part of town blacks could live in. Elsewhere in town, when they found out she was black, "the first thing they'd say was that [the house] was sold."

Independently or collectively, poverty, cultural difference, and skin color inspired stigma. Buckner-Webb remembered hearing it time and again: "'That's where the colored people live; that's where the so-and-so-live.' I say, 'Hate to disappoint you or disprove your ignorance, but look at the census records.'"

Neighborhood Business

Neighborhood grocery store owners and entrepreneurs must have felt every inch "blue-collar" as they struggled long hours as sole proprietors of neighborhood-supported stores south of the tracks. John Phillips, white businessman and long-time Lee Street resident, was a driver for Falk's department store in 1908, then owned neighborhood Pearl Grocery from 1917 to 1930. White businessman Roland Crisp eventually acquired the Pearl and later established Grand Avenue Market, a laundromat, and other businesses on South 12th and Grand north of Ash and Lee. Other neighborhood grocery stores included Zurcher's and Brown's, but all succumbed when K-Mart arrived in the late 1960s and settled nearby on newly gentrified, reclaimed river-bottom land. Doris Thomas recalled that when the big store drove the small ones out, without a car she could no longer conveniently walk to a laundromat or grocery store.

On Pioneer Street, enterprising Luther Johnson collected rent and looked after property for white landlords renting to black and white tenants south of the tracks. "Because many people didn't want to be bothered dealing with 'those folks,' they would hire him to collect the rent," said Cherie Buckner-Webb of her grandfather. Her grandmother ran a boarding house on Miller. Together, the Johnsons saw business opportunities and took advantage of them in a time and a tough place where success was the result of one's own making.

Residents were at home on their streets and knew the importance of being good neighbors. They were forthright about their jobs and took pride in what they did for a living as domestic and restaurant workers, cooks, bartenders, clerks, and store owners. Doris Thomas raised her family by waitressing from the 1930s to the 1970s. Her husband earned $3 a day working 12-hour days, covered their rent, and finally bought a house. "We didn't ever make a lot of money, but we didn't go into debt," Doris recalled.

Decline of the Neighborhood

What was left standing along Miller, Ash, Lee, and Grand in the 1950s has been gradually removed and replaced

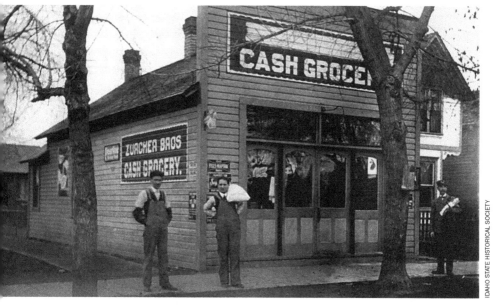

Zurcher's Cash Grocery
on South 13th Street

with low-income housing, empty lots, and commercial development, obliterating the integrity and history of this culturally unique neighborhood.

Removal, replacement, and alterations to residences occurred throughout the River Street neighborhood's history so that by 1980, much of the streetscape and residential area had been removed. Deconstruction proceeds inexorably: Ash Street is now devoid of all but one of its original dwellings, all lost to street realignments, commercial conversion, multi-unit housing endeavors, and lot leveling.

Longtime residents saw their small neighborhood deteriorate and blamed decline on landlords who failed to maintain properties or carefully screen new tenants. Longtime residents felt that "outsiders" brought trouble with them. Renters came and went, establishing no ties with their neighbors and leaving property in disrepair.

Warehouses, traffic, commercial-size blocks and their delivery-friendly street grids, and vacated industrial real estate persist in 2016. The trains are now missing, as are whole residential blocks overwhelmed by decades of sharing the neighborhood with steel, concrete, cinder block, and noise.

A 60-year-old trailer park occupies the southeast edge of the neighborhood. With the orderly layout of trailers along Lee and South 11th, steel and aluminum multi-unit housing was introduced to the neighborhood more than 30 years before the four concrete-and-brick-box apartment buildings were stacked on Ash and Lee. The trailer park remains much as it was in the 1950s.

The historic neighborhood is riddled with landlord-leveled lots slowly being walled in by concrete warehouses that squat on the edges. Trucks load in the alley. If their bulk is out of sight for some in the neighborhood, their diesel fumes and noise confirm their industrial presence.

Proposed city redevelopment plans to preserve the remnants died. House by house, the Lee and Ash grid is disintegrating and disappearing as homes are leveled, landscaping is scraped clean, and lawns are stripped bare of grass and shrubs. The one remaining constant, imperturbable in its concrete and asphalt presence, is the street configuration.

Long-silent voices expressed concern for their neighborhood's future well-being more than 35 years ago. Years of photo inventories reveal the rise and decline of property integrity. What urban renewal triggered in surrounding neighborhoods more than 40 years ago, landlords are vying for on the streets of Ash and Lee. With no architectural integrity of structures or setting, a new neighborhood is clearly the future here. Those along Ash and Lee who struggle to make a living will be forced to move elsewhere whether they can afford to or not.

PAM DEMO is a long-time Boisean. This chapter is based on her 2006 master's thesis, "Boise's River Street Neighborhood: Ash, Lee, & Lovers Lane/ Pioneer Streets – The South Side of the Tracks."

Hard Times at Chula Vista

Braceros made community in Wilder's migrant camps.

10

by Anna Webb

Issues of the *Wilder Herald* from the late 1930s and 1940s in Idaho depict an agricultural town concerned with what one might expect: news of the harvest, society notes about citizens traveling here or there or passing on to the great beyond. There are photographs of new brides headed for lives on nearby farmsteads. There are recipes, lists of local boys serving in the wartime military, and ads for swank hotels in Salt Lake City. One article details a collision between a calf and a car that resulted in more damage to the car than the calf. The story made the paper, which says something about the nature of life in Wilder at that time.

Other writings, news reports, and oral histories reveal different narratives—stories of hardscrabble times, tough work, and transient populations that represented a more ethnic and geographic diversity than that typically associated with Idaho.

Wilder is located between the Boise and Snake rivers in the western part of Canyon County. Vast swaths of sagebrush dominated the landscape until homesteaders, anticipating the arrival of irrigation, settled there in 1904.

Like other rural communities in Idaho and elsewhere, Wilder was home to Depression-era labor camps. Over the decades, the camps, some privately owned, some owned and operated by the federal government, housed a variety of people with very different backgrounds, but who had certain circumstances in common: poverty, need, and, frequently, marginalization.

The Farm Security Administration (FSA) founded the Wilder Labor Camp on the western outskirts of town. By 1941, the mobile camp was thriving and attracting workers from across the United States. The camp began as an optimistic place, a harbor for American families fleeing the dust bowl. These families sought literally greener pastures.

In later years, the camp was home to Braceros (Mexican workers) brought in to stem the wartime labor shortage, then to Japanese Americans newly released from internment camps, then to generations of migrant workers. A reinvention of the camp

DOROTHEA LANGE (U.S. FARM SECURITY ADMINISTRATION)

in the mid-1970s into Chula Vista Acres, a project of the Wilder Housing Authority, was in some ways a return to those earlier, more hopeful times of the New Deal.

The former labor camp is emblematic of similar camps that never closed down or went away, but that were continually inhabited and reinvented.

Today, Chula Vista Acres is a 30-acre complex of tan duplexes located at Wilder's western edge on Idaho State Highway 19. It's home to 95 families. Most are of Mexican descent. Most of the residents are employed in agriculture. Most live at Chula Vista year round in a city that is now 75% Latino.

In Search of a Better Life

Chula Vista's roots were in the New Deal. The FSA and its predecessor, the Resettlement Administration, were New Deal programs created to help poor farmers and their families weather two overwhelming challenges: the dust bowl and the Great Depression. Beginning in the late 1930s, the FSA built 34 government-owned labor camps, including those in the Idaho towns of Wilder, Caldwell (which today is Farmway Village), Ola, and Shelley. The camps were intended as rural reform measures, havens for desperate people. The camps were tools for "social rehabilitation," wrote Erasmo Gamboa in his book, *Mexican Labor and World War II: Braceros in the Pacific Northwest, 1942-1947.*

In Mountain Shadows: A History of Idaho, by Carlos A. Schwantes, includes an observation by Senator William Borah about itinerant farmers of that era in search of a better life. "Drive out on any of the main highways of our state and you will see cars, sometimes almost caravans, fleeing from the devastations of the drought."

As great experiments in communal living, the government farms provided work for struggling farm laborers. They also offered community amenities like shower rooms, laundry facilities, medical clinics, grocery stores, and more. The Wilder FSA camp and others like it became stopping places for families that took on the now less than politically correct appellations "Okie" and "Arkie" for their roots in the American South. The narrative of "dust bowl migrants" spread through popular culture. The Joad family, central to John Steinbeck's *The Grapes of Wrath*, striving to better their lot in life, found shelter in government labor camps.

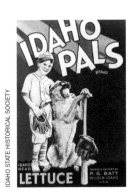

Advertisement for Batt brand lettuce

Wilder native and former Idaho Governor Phil Batt recalled in a 2015 interview his father's farm and the work crew that joined Batt and other family members in the fields before the war. "Dad had a 10-man crew who worked year round. Okies and Arkies," said Batt. "Dad loved them and had a lot of good things to say about where they had come from. Most brought their families. They were a good community."

Oral histories offer more details about life in the Wilder labor camps. The California State College, Bakersfield Oral History Project includes an interview from 1981 with Bobby Glenn Russell, the son of a family from Arkansas who traveled west in the 1930s in search of work. Russell's reminiscences included Idaho (and Wilder) as one stop on a long, rough path through the West. "We learned early that there were fruit tramps, cotton tramps and pea tramps. Each group had their own trail. There were gathering points for slack seasons. The pea tramps would hit Edison (California) then go into Oregon, Washington and over into Wilder, Idaho then back down through Santa Maria and winter in Brawley and Calipatria (California). It was just a run they made. They'd fill in picking strawberries."

The Idaho State Archives and Research Center houses the oral history of Wilder resident Glenn Osborn, who served as the city's chief of police, public works superintendent, and fire chief. Osborn's own family came to Idaho from Missouri in 1938 during the Great Depression, lured by the promise of "an abundance of food in Idaho." Osborn recalls Wilder's labor camps, "tents and shacks" inhabited by "Okies and Arkies" who worked 10-hour days in the fields for 10 to 15 cents an hour.

Once its camps were up and running, the Farm Security Administration needed to show the public that its programs were successful and that its farm labor camps were, as intended, providing support for large numbers of struggling

Americans. The agency hired photographers to travel across the United States to document American life, including life in the camps, in the largest photography project ever sponsored by the U.S. government. The project, which some said showed America at its most vulnerable, is arguably the

Migrant farmer

most lasting legacy of the Farm Security Administration. The photo project cemented the careers of photographers such as Dorothea Lange, Walker Evans, Arthur Rothstein, and others. Bold black and white images showed Americans what the Great Depression looked like. Images of Idaho are among the comprehensive photo collections (publicly available and searchable online) held by the Library of Congress and Yale University.

Chicago-born Russell Lee was the FSA photographer who traveled to Idaho to document camp life in Wilder and other Idaho communities in 1941. Lee's photographs of Wilder reveal people living modest lives but lives that were also undeniably hopeful and forward-looking: a worker watering down the dusty ground near his tent; farm workers unloading their belongings into the tent where they would live; doctors and nurses in crisp white in "trailer clinics," tending to farm

Child living in the migratory labor camp

Russell Lee promotes the FSA resettlement program, Wilder, 1941.

workers' children; the interior of a farm worker's car strung with good luck trinkets. Lee's caption for the photograph of the tent notes that the tents had floors. The fact that farm workers had running water, a community building for entertainment, and other benefits, Lee remarked, made it a better place to live than the tents might have suggested.

After photographing FSA labor camps in Wilder, Caldwell, and other Idaho communities, Lee continued his work in the West, documenting Japanese American internment at Camp Minidoka, now a national monument.

The World Comes to Wilder

The outbreak of World War II meant that some white itinerant farm workers left the labor camps to join the war effort. Others found more lucrative jobs in urban wartime factories. This created an urgent labor shortage for American farm owners. New populations of workers moved into labor camps in Wilder and elsewhere to fill the gap.

Wilder Herald articles from 1943 mention "Gypsy pea pickers" who organized a strike for better wages. Phil Batt remembered Jamaicans working the fields in Wilder. Glenn Osborn recalled Puerto Ricans working in Wilder during the same era. German prisoners of war, too, were held in a Wilder labor camp east of town. An article from the *Spokesman-Review* from 1945 tells of three German soldiers ranging in age from 19 to 22 who escaped from the camp. The Federal Bureau of Investigation reported that the men were caught not 24 hours after escaping.

Wilder's camps also housed Braceros (literally "strong-armed men"), who were part of a U.S. program to bring Mexican agricultural workers to the Northwest to work in food production beginning in 1943. Historian Gamboa said it was common for Braceros to move into FSA camps, although they were frequently segregated. The mission of the camps, too, had shifted, from providing social support and rural rehabilitation for poor American laborers to providing lodging for workers to ease the way for American farm owners who needed cheap labor.

The production of food was vital to the war effort. But the fact that they were performing vital work did not guarantee good conditions for Braceros. Schwantes wrote in his book *The Pacific Northwest: An Interpretive History*, "Migrants complained about living conditions: their housing often amounted to little more than tents in the winter and their food was often spoiled or dust covered, as was the case in a mess tent in Wilder, Idaho, where strong winds blasted through the facility and seasoned the food with grit."

Phil Batt, former governor of Idaho

The social climate was, it seems, a mix of discrimination and indifference. As a Wilder native born in 1918 into a farm family, Phil Batt was in a unique position to witness both sentiments. Batt was known throughout his political career for his human rights advocacy. As a Republican governor (1995-1999), he advocated for the state to recognize Martin Luther King's birthday, an unpopular position at the time. As a state senator in the late 1960s, he held informal hearings on minority issues in Idaho. He also pushed, successfully, for the legislature to establish the Idaho Commission on Human Rights.

Public Television featured an interview with Batt as part of *The Color of Conscience*, a series produced by Marcia Franklin in 2011. Franklin asked him about his hometown. "There were a few people who were definitely racist, and one of them would be a store-keeper who had a sign, 'No Dogs or Mexicans' in his window," said Batt. "Of course that was disturbing to most of us. For the most part I don't think the people thought much about race at all. They just thought their own insular affairs were what dictated their lives."

The Mexican government refused to send workers to Idaho because of the discrimination, abuse, and poor living and working conditions. The U.S. government discontinued the Bracero program in Idaho in 1948. The FSA farm labor camp program had also wound down by then. Camps across the United States came under the governance of local entities, including, in some cases, farmers associations. The Wilder Farm Labor Sponsoring Committee took over the former FSA camp and a second camp known as the West Valley Camp. Individual farmers also continued to build and run private labor camps on their property.

The end of the Bracero program in Idaho did not mean the end of Mexican workers coming to Wilder and other rural communities. Instead, more migrant workers, and eventually their families, came to the area independently of the Bracero program and made their temporary homes at the labor camps.

By the mid-1960s, according to the governor's *Report on Idaho Migratory Labor Camps*, 13 camps were operating within a roughly 10-mile radius around Wilder. These reports noted a variety of living conditions for workers. Some camps were well-kept. But in many cases, the conditions were poor, including lack of running water and adequate waste disposal.

Hard Work and Strong Community

"El campo de Wilder. It was crazy," said Arnold Hernandez, now director of multicultural affairs at the College of Idaho. Hernandez came to Wilder with his family in 1969 when he was 10 years old. The family moved into the Wilder Labor Camp. "We came from South Texas. A compadre of my dad's said, 'You know what, if you go to El Norte, there will be work there for you and your whole family.' We had no idea where we were going," said Hernandez.

His recollection of camp life included a mix of the grim and the good. The Wilder Labor Camp, he said, seemed like a large family with everyone living together in small quarters with a vital social sphere that included good food, music, and gossip. But he also recalls mattresses infested with bed bugs and roads filled with potholes and mud. Residents who were

Braceros pick potatoes, 1944.

new to the camp and had no seniority lived in barracks made from old train cars. Hernandez recalled cinder block showers and a communal bathroom in poor repair. "When ladies went to the restroom, they always took someone with them who could stand in front of the holes in the wall to give them some privacy," said Hernandez.

Poverty was rampant in the Wilder Labor Camp, he said. "But at the same time, we didn't know what poverty was. To us life in the camp was richness, culture and families. After a while, everyone becomes extended family around the labor camp."

A Mexican pea-picker pauses for a photograph with his children at migrant camp in Idaho's Teton County.

Hernandez and other children living at the camp worked in the fields along with their parents and older relatives. Children wore big hats, coats, and baggy pants to look bigger and older. "Some of those rows of beets and onions were a quarter of a mile long. We would work the far end of the rows so the farmer who owned the fields couldn't see how young we were," said Hernandez.

Trips to Caldwell for Mexican dances were one of the highlights of camp life, Hernandez said. "You'd get KFC," he recalled. "You'd dance with young ladies. The next day you'd be working in the fields, talking to your friends about the girls. 'They were crying all over me,' you'd say. 'Yeah, they were crying alright,' your friends would say, 'because you smelled like onions.'"

For some years, Hernandez and his family lived the typical migrant lifestyle, returning to Texas during the winter or traveling for agricultural work in Oregon and Washington. The family eventually settled permanently in Wilder. When Hernandez turned 16, he left school to work full-time in the fields. He was fortunate to get another job working for a bookmobile that traveled from labor camp to labor camp. That second job, he said, changed his life. He impressed his bosses, who immediately recognized that he was a smart kid. "Someone saw something in me," Hernandez said. "They told me I was college material."

Hernandez studied and got his GED in a mere 2½ weeks. He enrolled in Boise State University with help from the College Assistance Migrant Program and majored in education. Now, as director of the multicultural program at College of Idaho, he works with students who have histories similar to his own, some with roots in Wilder and at Chula Vista.

Beginnings of Reform

Raquel Reyes was born in the 1960s and raised in Wilder. She now works as the grant specialist for the Community Council of Idaho, formerly the Idaho Migrant Council, founded in 1971. The Community Council provides an array of social programs, including migrant Head Start, medical clinics, housing assistance (mostly in eastern Idaho), job training, and career counseling for farm workers who want to transition out of the fields into professions with better pay and opportunities for advancement.

Her father, the late Ramiro Reyes, a community leader and minister, began migrating to Idaho for work in agriculture in the 1950s. He founded Iglesia Evangelica, a bilingual, bicultural church in Wilder in 1962. In later years, Reyes worked to improve living conditions for migrants.

The 1960s was an era when some reforms were beginning to take place in support of migrant laborers. In 1956, local religious organizations formed the Southern Idaho Migrant Ministry. In 1955, the Idaho State Legislature created the Governor's Migratory Labor Committee. Both organizations were concerned with improving the lives of migrants, including improving their housing in labor camps.

The Reyes family was among the first former migrant families to buy a home in Wilder. Raquel Reyes did not live at the Wilder Labor Camp when she was a child, but her best friend lived there. Reyes visited often. "I remember the cinder block cabins. A family of seven living in a two-room brick cabin. You walked into what was the kitchen area. There would be a two-burner gas stove on top of the counter and a sink. You'd walk through a hallway into a makeshift bedroom/livingroom/gathering place," said Reyes.

Like Hernandez, she recalled barracks made from train cars. "You just took it for granted that that was the way those families lived. It never dawned on me that my friend's house was different from my house, but I can tell you the housing was very poor. Very hot in the summer with no ventilation and very cold in the fall before the people left."

In 1971 San Antonio's Bishop Patricio Flores visited Idaho. In Spanish, he told a crowd of 175 at St. Paul's Catholic Church in Nampa that migrants should stay put and pressure their newly adopted communities to provide them with education, housing, and health care. "The monkeys in the San Antonio zoo have better places to live than the migrants in Texas or in Idaho." Flores informed his audience that "even the Church will not begin to listen" until migrants and ex-migrants demand inclusion on an equal basis.

From Minority to Majority

In 1972, the City of Wilder passed a resolution to establish a housing authority. The city annexed the Wilder Labor Camp. In 1975, the housing authority secured a grant and a bond from the U.S. Department of Agriculture (USDA) to tear down the labor camp and rebuild the complex as affordable family housing for agricultural workers. The USDA package also included funds for rental assistance for tenants.

The city named the complex *Chula Vista* (Spanish for "beautiful view"). Crews razed the cinder block cabins and hauled away the train car barracks. The complex was rebuilt in two phases, in 1976 and 1979, said David Lincoln, housing authority administrator. Improvements included paved roads, grassy common areas, a community center, and a new water and sewer system.

Although the history of Chula Vista was typical of other camps in many ways, the improvements to its physical plant

Concrete blocks housed migrant labor before the rebuilding of Chula Vista.

set it somewhat apart. A 1980 report by an Idaho advisory committee to the U.S. Commission on Civil Rights looked at migrant housing across southern Idaho. The report found migrant housing, in general, "deplorable." But Chula Vista—with its 80 individual two- and three-bedroom houses furnished with beds, dressers, tables, chairs, full stoves, and refrigerators—fared relatively well in the report.

"The Chula Vista complex is not recognizable as farm labor housing, although it sits directly on the road entering town," read the report. "Their choice of names was a careful and deliberate one, reflecting an attempt to create a planned community atmosphere rather than perpetuate the traditional 'labor camp' image."

The complex, according to the report, had year-round occupancy and maintained a waiting list. A community center provided space for tenant gatherings on the main floor and a child care program in the basement. "Many persons recommended Wilder's operation as an example of what farmworker housing could (and should) be," the report continued.

Chula Vista is unique in another way. In 2012, the complex, now 120 units, paid off its debt to the USDA. "We're independent. We're running on our own," said Lincoln.

Ismael Fernandez, a college freshman, serves on Wilder's all-Latino city council.

The transition came with challenges. Paying off the debt meant an end to USDA rent subsidies. Chula Vista lost a third of its residents who could no longer afford to live there. The complex struggled for a couple years to fill its vacancies, said Lincoln, but today, the complex is full. As of 2016, rent for a two-bedroom duplex, including utilities, was $470.

The association with the USDA required residents to work in agriculture. That requirement is gone, said Lincoln, but in this overwhelmingly rural community, nearly all of Chula Vista's current residents still work in agricultural professions. Less than 10% of residents migrate during the winter. Farm work, particularly in hops production (an industry that is expanding because of all the new local breweries), is available all year. During the off-season, some residents work in onion and apple packing operations. Others find work in local meat processing and fertilizer plants.

Wilder's Mexican American community, too, continues to establish itself in the Canyon County mainstream, a far cry from the early days of the Bracero program and the signs in shop windows banning Mexicans. A majority of Wilder residents are Latino. In 2015, the city elected its first all-Latino city council as well as its first Latina (and first female) mayor, Alicia Almazan. The election was notable enough to warrant an article in the *Huffpost*.

Seventy-five percent of the 450 students enrolled in Wilder's public school system live in Chula Vista Acres. The school district is one of the poorest in the state with nearly all of its students qualifying for free and reduced lunch. "Chula Vista is still a place that needs help," said Lincoln. For a time the Idaho Foodbank made deliveries directly to the complex's community center. "But it's no longer a hard luck place." There's reason for optimism, Lincoln added. The Wilder School District was a recent recipient of an Apple ConnectED grant that will provide an iPad for each student in the district.

Although the people who originally came to Chula Vista were passing through in tough circumstances, Chula Vista is changing from a transient place to a stable neighborhood. Wilder, in turn, has transformed in many ways, and Latinos are becoming the mainstream of the town rather than a marginalized class.

NPR.ORG

Wilder mayor, Alicia Mora Almazan, receives a congratulatory hug after her swearing-in ceremony.

ANNA WEBB is a Boise native. She is a reporter at the *Idaho Statesman* and has written on a variety of historic topics, including the Spanish flu epidemic, Japanese internment camps, and Boise history in her book *150 Boise Icons*, which marked the city's sesquicentennial.

A Hard Places Driving Tour

Todd Shallat and Molly Humphreys, with John Bertram

Austere places of repellent beauty are the most ordinary of American landscapes yet the most disdained and misunderstood. In a society that cherishes wealth, equating success with virtue, memories repress misfortune. Historic preservation can contribute to that memory loss. In Ada and Canyon counties, of the esteemed 201 "historically significant" sites on the National Register of Historic Places, only hay barns and a Boise dairy recall the manual toil of everyday lives. Two-thirds of those National Register listings are mansions, mausoleums, and banks. No plaques memorialize migrant housing. None recall the irrigators without irrigation, the paupers remanded to poor farms, or the whiskey-and-morphine districts where risk-takers gambled and lost.

This driving tour features 24 alternative sites. Recovered from history's void, most meet the National Register's criteria for historic places, being older than 50 years and "associated with events that have made a significant contribution to the broad patterns of our history." We group them loosely by type: the *forgotten* places, nearly lost to community memory; the *neglected* places, too common for veneration; and the *misunderstood* places, remembered in ways that obscure the darker side.

Tour maps (pp. 131-133) mark the woeful places on a valleywide driving tour.

The Forgotten

① Levy's Alley, Boise

UCLA

"CRIB GIRL," 1897

Downtown alleys from 6th to 9th, between Main and Idaho streets, now mostly occupied by city hall

Prostitution flourished in downtown Boise before and during the gold rush era. In the 1890s, prostitutes rented small rooms and shanty "cribs" behind about 20 saloons on Main Street. Levy's Alley, named after a notorious brothel landlord, anchored the east end of the district on the block now occupied by Boise City Hall. Women's temperance organizations worked with Boise mayors to eradicate prostitution by closing saloons. Boise's temperance fountain, dedicated in 1910, stands on the northwest corner of City Hall Plaza as a reminder of the anti-saloon, anti-prostitution crusade.

② Orchard Town Site, Ada County

MOLLY HUMPHREYS

ORCHARD SCHOOLHOUSE

At the junction of the Union Pacific Main Line Railroad and Orchard Access Road, east of Boise and 4 miles south of the Boise Stage Stop off I-84

In 1883, with the coming of the Oregon Short Line, two speculators established a fruit ranch and invested in an ill-fated reservoir and canal from Indian Creek. Water rights were advertised, prune trees and potatoes were planted, and in 1895 the town site of Orchard was platted and registered with Ada County. Drought and dust had forced most homesteaders from the town site by the time the railroad rerouted the main line in 1925. Today only a rail crossing, clapboard schoolhouse, and steel water tower remain.

③ Hendrickson Shootout, Boise County

MOLLY HUMPHREYS

PEARL ROYAL
HENDRICKSON
1890 — 1940

HENDRICKSON'S HEADSTONE

About 50 yards off Boise Ridge Road north of Eagleson Summit, approximately 10 miles north of the Boise Barracks

On July 31, 1940, in a small cabin on U.S. Forest Service land near Bogus Basin, a posse of at least 50 men gunned down homesteader Pearl Royal Hendrickson. African American, he had been a WWI combat doughboy before retreating to his foothills homestead. Well liked, he watched after open-range livestock, tended a garden, and survived mostly on bear meat. In 1936, when the Forest Service sectioned off his homestead for Bogus Basin, Hendrickson went to court and eventually lost title to his homestead claim.

Hendrickson, in protest, barricaded the homestead with scrap metal from abandoned cars. He shot and killed the first two federal marshals sent to evict him. FBI agents, sheriffs, state police, and prison guards with machine guns laid siege and opened fire. Hendrickson kept them at bay for 4 hours with a single rifle. Wounded but captured alive, he died en route to a Boise hospital. A headstone marks his grave in Morris Hill Cemetery.

④ Five Mile Cemetery, Meridian

HOMESTEADER HEADSTONES

At 2400 W. San Remo Court, off W. Ustick Road via Towerbridge Way

Seven graves on a tiny plot in an upscale subdivision mark the misfortune of homesteaders cut short in life. Enclosed by the Meridian's BridgeTower subdivision, the cemetery recalls the heyday of dry farming along Five Mile Creek.

Only two of the seven lived past their 40th birthday. In 1883, Hercules Young of Missouri arrived with his wife to farm 120 acres. He patented the land in 1889 but died the following year. Brothers George and Samuel Nisbet, also emigrants from Missouri, filed claim on nearby homesteads. Samuel died at age 35, less than 6 months after receiving his homestead patent. George received his patent after his death at age 40. The brothers share a single marker. Nina McGinnis, daughter of area homesteaders, is the youngest resident of the Five Mile Cemetery. She died at age 13.

---

⑤ Riverside Hooverville, 8th Street, Boise

HOOVERVILLE SHANTY

West of the 8th Street Bridge, on the banks of the Boise River

In the 1930s, in the depth of the Great Depression, the homeless built tarpaper shantytowns near depots and rail yards. Called "Hoovervilles" in disdain for President Herbert Hoover, they housed the evicted and dispossessed.

In Boise they clustered in encampments near bridges where abutments and levees stabilized the wandering floodplain. Residents were mostly young men—"not hoboes," said a railroad official quoted in the *Idaho Statesman*, "just boys who don't know where they are going nor why." Smaller camps dotted the junglelike hollows hidden by willows and brush.

Hoovervilles swelled in Boise as the average income of Idahoans, from 1929 to 1933, plunged by 50%. New Dealers responded with farm relief, construction projects, and 270 Idaho camps for 80,000 workers under the supervision of FDR's Civilian Conservation Corps.

---

⑥ German POW Camp, Upper Deer Flat, Canyon County

SURRENDERING POW

At the junction of S. Powerline and Deer Flat Road, east of State Highway 45, south of the New York Canal

Only a shack remains of the Upper Deer Flat camp, one of six in southwestern Idaho. In all, 18 Idaho "branch camps" radiated from the War Department's prison compound near Paul. German soldiers captured in combat worked for Idaho farmers under light security. Inmates slept in tents on a cement pad on the Swartz farm south of Nampa where the Upper Deer Flat Branch Camp was located in May 1945. Another branch camp held prisoners near the junction of Franklin Boulevard and Ustick Road.

The Neglected

⑦ *Morris Hill Cemetery, Boise*

MOLLY HUMPHREYS

MORRIS HILL CEMETERY

At 317 N. Latah, off Emerald Street on the South Depot Bench

Mayor James Pinney signed City Ordinance 60 in June 1883, officially establishing Morris Hill Cemetery. Elaborate crypts mark the graves of the wealthy. Paupers share the mostly anonymous Ada County section near the cemetery's northeast corner along Emerald Street. Dozens were hastily buried during the 1918 flu pandemic. Many were enclosed in wooden coffins and planted under slabs of hand-etched concrete. Other graves were simply unmarked.

---

⑧ *Idaho State School and Hospital, Nampa*

IDAHO BUSINESS REVIEW

STATE SCHOOL AND HOSPITAL

At 1660 11th Avenue North, off I-84

This facility, located on the outskirts of Nampa, was established in 1911 as the Nampa State School and Colony to house profoundly mentally and physically disabled children. When Whitehall Dormitory opened in 1918, there were 40 residents. However, once admitted to the institution it was almost guaranteed that a child would never leave. Eventually the State School and Colony became a warehouse for the severely disabled of any age, and dormitories were filled substantially beyond capacity.

Institution directors recommended sterilization of the mentally incapacitated to prevent them from producing any more social misfits. The Idaho Legislature passed this into law in 1925 and sterilizations began at the hospital in 1931. What they did not pass was sufficient funding for adequate staff, building maintenance, or new construction. By 1956, more than 900 severely challenged residents were residing in cramped dormitories stacked in bunk beds sometimes three high. Whitehall was on the verge of being condemned in the 1960s after the roof collapsed several times and the urine-rotted wood floors of the upper-story wards started to sag. Initially, residents were simply moved to the bottom floor. Eventually they were rehoused in other buildings or sent to State Hospital North in Orofino.

---

⑨ *Overland Trailer Park, Boise*

IDAHO BUSINESS REVIEW

FIRE-RAVAGED MOBILE HOME

At 5615 Overland Road

Boise's first trailer park was established in 1947 near the corner of Curtis and Overland roads as affordable housing for returning soldiers at the close of World War II. Since that time, it has been home to the poor, disabled, elderly, and recent immigrants with limited English speaking ability, all members of the community that are often ignored.

In the early winter of 2006, as the temperatures dipped into the freezing zone, the City of Boise threatened to cut power to the park because of the imminent fire danger posed by an electrical system that had not been updated since the park was established. The problem was identified when a couple was found living in a burned-out shell of a trailer earlier that fall. The park owner was given 5 days to initiate the repairs or residents would be evicted. Many residents owned their homes and planned to stay even if the power was shut off. The trailers were from the 1970s or earlier and too old to move. If residents abandoned their homes, they would be left with nothing.

---

⑩ *Abandoned Mines at Pearl, Gem County*

GEM COUNTY HISTORICAL SOCIETY

PEARL, IDAHO, 1902

Pearl Road, off State Highway 55 south of Horseshoe Bend, about 8 miles southeast of Emmett

Hard times in the hard rock mines were what most hopeful miners experienced when they arrived in the developing town of Pearl in the late 1890s. Wages were the equivalent of $10 to $11 in today's market, but the work was extremely demanding and often incredibly dangerous. Rising early, miners spent most of their working hours in the damp, dark mines. On a daily basis miners were exposed to toxic cyanide leaching compounds that caused suffocation and lung disease. Extremely sensitive nitroglycerine blasting compounds emitted significant amounts of carbon monoxide that, if handled improperly, poisoned miners in the shaft. Accidents resulting from falling rock, dynamite blasts, and electrocution were not uncommon.

After a heyday between 1900 and 1907, the town of Pearl began to decline. The large mines began to sink due to the massive amounts of subsurface material removed and profits began to plummet. By the 1970s all active mining operations had come to a halt. Today one can see mining adits, wooden remains of mills, and scarred hillsides, all that remains of the once booming town of Pearl.

⑪ *Coaling Station at Nampa Train Depot, Nampa*

LIBRARY OF CONGRESS

NAMPA COALING STATION

At 1200 Front Street, off 12th Avenue

Some 250,000 American teenagers rode the rails in search of work during the Great Depression. Many were rousted and arrested at the coaling depot in Nampa en route to Yakima or La Grange. "I still feel the sting of a cop's billy club beating on the bottom of my soles from snoozing in a RR station to keep warm," said Bill Bender, a hobo in 1937.

Peggy Easton of Wyoming, arrested for vagrancy, recalled her escape from Nampa after a cold night in jail. "The bulls [railroad police] were patrolling the area with rifles and lanterns. . . . When the engine started up a wave of bums rose up like one person and rushed for that open door. I was the first one there. Someone behind me picked me up by the nape of neck and the seat of the pants and pitched me into the car."

⑫ *Convict Quarries, Boise*

IDAHO STATE HISTORICAL SOCIETY

QUARRYING STONE

At 2150 Old Penitentiary Road, off Warm Springs Avenue

Bad men made good roads, according to the prison officials who hoped to profit from prison labor. Idaho needed gravel and sandstone. Its territorial prison fronted the Boise hillside with strata of marblelike stone. In 1893 convicts uncovered a boneyard of "grinning skeletons" said to be Indian graves. Prison labor cut stone in 20-inch blocks for stately landmarks—for Boise City National Bank (1891), the Union Block (1901), and hundreds of Queen Anne layer cake homes. In 1906, with work beginning on the Idaho Statehouse, prisoners expanded the quarry under Table Rock Butte. Broken stone from the original quarry flanks an interpretive trail above the ward for notorious women at the Old Idaho Penitentiary Museum.

⑬ Women's and Children's Alliance, Boise

ANDREW CRISP, BOISE WEEKLY

WCA "TAKING FLIGHT" STATUE

At 720 W. Washington Street

A butterfly of stained glass takes flight from the outstretched hand of a young mother with children in the bronze sculpture in the shadow of the Idaho Statehouse. The sculpture fronts a crisis center that shelters victims of rape and domestic abuse. Founded by church congregations in 1910, the Young Women's Christian Association (YWCA) of Boise began as a cafeteria and social haven for young ladies in an uncouth city. In 1940, the association moved to Washington Street, and gradually the mission expanded into a women and children's shelter. In 1996, the name changed to the Women's and Children's Alliance (WCA).

---

⑭ Oregon Short Line Rail Bridge, Boise

JOEL SLAGG

RAILROAD BRIDGE, 1985

At the river along the Boise Greenbelt just west of Shoreline Drive

About 250 young men from Japan worked near Boise on the Oregon Short Line in the decade of Idaho's statehood. Three-man teams lifted lava rocks onto flatcars for levees and bridge abutments. Quarantined for fear of smallpox, they slept outside the city in trackside camps and boxcars. Japanese road gangs, in 1893, completed the two timber trusses that bridged the railroad onto an island and into downtown. A steel structure replaced the wooden truss in 1923.

---

⑮ Old Ada County Jail, Boise

ADA COUNTY

CELL AT THE COURTHOUSE JAIL

At 514 W. Jefferson Street, now the top floor of the Boise campus of the University of Idaho Law School

Ada County's original jail and courthouse faced Jefferson Street at 6th in 1867. Prisoners used buckets for toilets and slept on straw mattresses on the barren floor. In 1925, the jail held 25 inmates, most of them awaiting their day in court for drinking whiskey during Prohibition.

In 1940, with New Deal labor and funding, the county topped its imposing new limestone courthouse with its austere rooftop jail. In 1980, Hollywood's Clint Eastwood used the jail as a set for a scene in the film *Bronco Billy*, shot mostly in Boise.

⑯ *Nampa Fire of 1909, Nampa*

LIBRARY OF CONGRESS

DOWNTOWN NAMPA, 1907

An entire city block fronting the depot, bounded by 12th and 13th avenues, Front and First streets

On Saturday afternoon, July 3, 1909, a stranger with a cigar accidentally set off the fireworks that ignited the devastation. Within 3 hours, the fire had scorched 25 stores and burned out 60 businesses—about half the business district. Few merchants had fire insurance to cover their loss.

When Nampa's volunteers began fighting the fire, the hose was coupled up and water turned on, but there was no pressure. In changing from wooden to iron pipes, disconnections had been made, rendering the system useless. After receiving a call for help, the Boise Fire Department loaded their equipment onto a special train and made the run to Nampa, a distance of 20 miles, in 18 minutes. Caldwell also answered the call. Although the fire devastated the buildings and businesses on that block, creating hardships, within a year most had been rebuilt.

---

⑰ *Notus Canal and Bridge, Caldwell*

RONALD VAN HOOK

BRIDGE AT CANYON CROSSING

At Canyon Crossing, where W. Plymouth Road spans the Boise River to join Old Highway 30

A deep-cut canal with an unreliable source of water gave false hope to settlers near Notus. Built from 1919, expanded in 1924, the canal tapped a shallow reservoir on the Payette River. In 1941, a Bureau of Reclamation powerhouse increased the flow with a system of pumps.

The original wagon bridge at Canyon Crossing replaced the ferry in 1886. A steel camelback truss improved the crossing for motor traffic in 1921.

---

⑱ *Chula Vista Acres, Wilder*

LIBRARY OF CONGRESS

FSA RESETTLEMENT CAMP
WILDER LABOR CAMP, 1941

Southern edge of Wilder, off 5th Street at Simplot Road

Labor camps sprung up throughout southern Idaho during the Great Depression. One of these was established by the Farm Security Administration on the western edge of Wilder to provide new opportunities for farmers and their families fleeing the dust bowl in the Midwest and South. The onset of World War II created a labor shortage, and the predominately white workers at the camp were replaced with Mexican, Jamaican, and Japanese workers. By 1943, the Wilder Labor Camp was the largest and most successful in the state. In the mid-1970s, the Wilder Housing Authority assumed control of the Wilder camp and reinvented it as Chula Vista Acres. Today most of the residents are Latinos working as farm laborers.

The Misunderstood

⑲ *Fort Boise Refugee Encampment, Boise*

FORT BOISE OFFICER'S QUARTERS

BOISE ARCHITECTURE PROJECT

Above the Boise Barracks, W. Fort Street, between 6th and Reserve

At the base of the Boise foothills, where the road climbed west toward Idaho City, the U.S. Army claimed land as contested as any on the Oregon Trail. Here in 1863 and 1864 more than 300 captured Shoshone endured bitter winters in a tent encampment. Enclosed for their own protection, they shivered and starved without adequate rations or blankets. Some died from tuberculosis. Some wandered away and were shot on sight. In 1865, the camp moved to Arrowrock on the Boise River where the dam now impounds the canyon. In 1867, some 200 refugees were corralled into wagons and shipped to Fort Hall.

More than a century passed before a lawsuit over a housing project uncovered the embarrassing truths. Historians discovered that no ratified treaty had ceded claim to the foothills. The City of Boise has since purchased a grassy hillside overlooking the army barracks that guarded the refugee camp.

⑳ *Erma Hayman House, Boise*

HAYMAN HOUSE

JOHN BERTRAM

At 617 Ash Street, off River Street

A squat square house of whitewashed sandstone stands among vacant lots in a district slated for urban renewal. To developers, it is land well suited for high-density infill. For preservationists, the small house on Ash Street is a solitary reminder of Jim Crow segregation in a city that, even now, remains too insular to appreciate how stigmas of race and class keep minorities marginalized.

Built in 1895, the Erma Hayman House fronts River Street in a vanishing "colored town" of blacks, Basques, and Slavic Europeans. Erma Hayman and her husband Lawrence purchased the house in 1950, when covenants barred people of color from housing north of Front Street. Erma—a clerk in downtown Boise, a beloved caretaker to neighbors and children—lived in the house for more than 50 years.

㉑ *Kuna Caves, Ada County*

ENTRANCE TO KUNA CAVES

GARY PAULSON

Half-mile south of Kuna Road, off Swan Falls Road

Mystery shrouds the snake-infested lava blister 2 miles south of Kuna. Once the entrance was marked by the graves of diphtheria victims. A small stone corral flanked a primitive stage-stop saloon.

Tales of travail abound. Nearby, according to legend, Indians killed a stage driver as he fled toward the stage stop. Another legend has two cowboys, exploring with ropes and lanterns, finding a full skeleton on an underground ledge. There is also the tale of the outlaw who buried $40,000 in gold-coin treasure, escaping through a secret exit. Allegedly that back door collapsed when dynamite shook a nearby construction site.

Today the caves are on public rangeland. A 35-foot steel-cage ladder makes the lava a popular underground party location.

㉒ Spanish Village, Boise

IDAHO STATE HISTORICAL SOCIETY

MULE PACKER'S CABIN

Off the canal behind the medical office plaza at Second and Main streets

A line of trees shades a downtown canal where elderly mule packers lived out their lives in a circle of cabins. Children imagined the tenants were dwarfs and called the place "tiny town." But the cabins had once been a depot for mule trains. Entrepreneur Jesus Urquides, its founder, had blazed a supply route to the Boise Basin during the 1863 gold rush. Born in Mexico and seasoned in the Sierra Nevadas, Urquides had employed about 20 Mexican or "Spanish" packers. After 1928, with the death of Urquides, his daughter Dolores Binnard cared for the last of the aging packers. Bulldozers razed the cabins to make room for parking in 1972.

㉓ Halverson Bar, Ada County

BOISE STATE UNIVERSITY

WILLIAM "DOC" HISON

Off-road about 3 miles east of Celebration Park in the Morley Nelson Snake River Birds of Prey National Conservation Area

Hard-living men built lava rock cabins on the north banks of the Snake River during the era of railroads. In 1896 a rail bridge at Guffey brought construction workers and sluice miners. Today the site seems forlorn. Among ruins reclaimed by the desert, in a rocky corner of Ada County cut off from motor traffic, it is hard to imagine the life of the loners who terraced the land, dug ditches, and sluiced fine grains of gold.

The most famous was the hermit William "Doc" Hison (aka Hisom). Half-black, half–Native American, a thin scrubby man with a sweet honest smile, Hison was called "Doc" for his skill as a healer of sick animals. His closest neighbors celebrated Hison's 94th birthday in Melba in 1944.

Today a BLM trail branches through the lava ruins of Hison cabin at a cove of the Snake River called Halverson Bar. Ditch irrigation run-off trickles into a pond, stocked for fishing with bluegill, called Halverson Lake.

㉔ The Curse of Billy Fong, Boise

IDAHO STATESMAN

BILLY FONG

At 706½ Front Street, now the Grove Hotel

Lore has it that Chinese miners somehow built a network of tunnels to connect their opium dens. But there were probably never more than 250 Chinese in downtown Boise and they had no need for tunnels. Businessmen, restaurant owners, apothecaries, doctors, and vegetable farmers, they first clustered in a laundry district near 8th Street. Moved in 1901 when Boise condemned their wooden buildings, they relocated two blocks to Front Street dissected by 7th (Capitol Boulevard).

A cook named Billy Fong became a symbol of that district when the Hip Sing Company hired him to occupy its empty building. He had become, said the *Idaho Statesman*, "the last Chinese in Boise." In June 1972, at age 84, he left the building just hours ahead of its demolition. Fong was not actually chased from Boise. Front Street was already abandoned. But more than 80 buildings had fallen to the frenzy of urban renewal, and some had been cultural landmarks. The devastation left surface parking and crippled commerce downtown.

Legend has it that Fong cursed the construction site as he boarded a bus for San Francisco. Eighteen years passed before the Grove Hotel reclaimed the lot.

Boise: Downtown

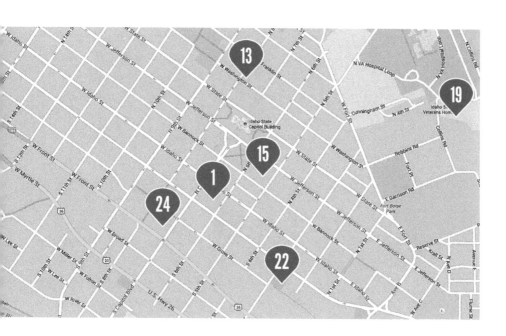

Boise: West of Downtown

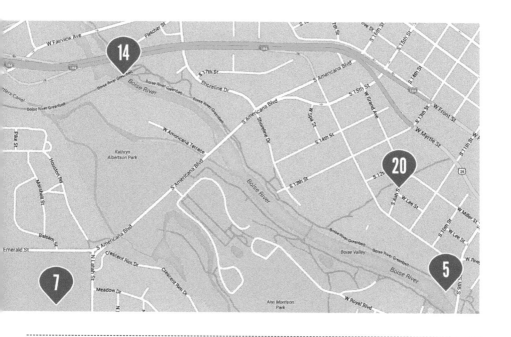

The Boise Valley

Credits and Sources

In the summer of 2015, in a downtown classroom, 10 sleuths and scholars-in-training began a search for stories of the underprivileged from history's bottom rung. Two professionals, two graduate students, and six undergraduates were the principal investigators. Todd Shallat, working with Colleen Brennan and Molly Humphreys, co-authored chapters 1, 3, 5, and 7, weaving threads into narrative prose. We gratefully acknowledge vital assistance from Steve Barrett, Amber Beierle, John Bertram, Kristof Bihari, Sarah Doering, Jenaleigh Kiebert, John Martinson, and Anna Webb.

Chapter 1: Boise's Forgotten Pandemic

Arrington, Leonard. "The Influenza Epidemic of 1918-1919 in Southern Idaho." *Idaho Yesterdays*, 32, no. 3 (1988): 19-29.

Arrington, Leonard. *History of Idaho*. 2 vols. Moscow: University of Idaho Press, 1994.

Beveridge, W. I. B. *Influenza: The Last Great Plague*. New York: Prodist, 1977.

Committee on the Atmosphere and Man. "Causes of Geographical Variation in the Influenza Epidemic." *National Research Council Bulletin*, 6, no. 34 (1923).

Crosby, Albert. *America's Forgotten Pandemic: The Influenza of 1918*. Cambridge, UK: Cambridge University Press, 1989.

Idaho Department of Health and Welfare. "1918-1919 Influenza Pandemic in Idaho." http://www.healthandwelfare. idaho.gov/Portals/0/Health/ReadyIdaho/IdahoFluHx.pdf

Idaho Statesman, 1918-1919.

Johnson, N. P., and Juergen Mueller. "Updating the Accounts: Global Mortality of the 1918-1920 'Spanish' Influenza Pandemic." *Bulletin of the History of Medicine* 76, no. 1 (2002): 105-115.

Kenner, Robert (Producer). "Influenza 1918." *American Experience* documentary series, Public Broadcasting System, 1998. www.pbs.org/wgbh/americanexperience

Reeves, R. S. "Cholangitis Following Influenza." *United States Naval Medical Bulletin* 13, no. 3 (1919): 557-558.

Reid, Ann, Jeffery Taubenberger, and Thomas Fanning. "The 1918 Spanish Influenza: Integrating History and Biology." *Microbes and Infection* 3, no. 1 (2001): 81-87.

Taubenberger, Jeffery, and David Morens. "1918 Influenza: The Mother of All Pandemics." *Emerging Infectious Diseases* 12, no. 1 (2006):15-22.

Chapter 2: Dollar a Day

Fujii, Henry. Oral history interview by Mary Henshall, November 24, 1973. Boise: Idaho State Archives and Research Center, Oral History Collection.

Hayashi, Robert T. *Haunted by Waters: A Journey through Race and Place in the American West*. Iowa City: University of Iowa Press, 2007.

Henshall, Mary. "Pioneer Portraits: Henry and Fumiko Fujii." *Idaho Yesterdays* (Spring 1975): 20-27.

Ichioka, Yuji. *The Issei: The World of the First Generation Japanese Immigrants 1885-1924*. New York: Free Press, 1988.

Idaho Statesman, 1892-1893.

Itō, Kazuo. *Issei: A History of Japanese Immigrants in North America*. Seattle, WA: Japanese Community Service, 1973.

"Japanese on the Move," *Caldwell Tribune*, July 30, 1892.

Mercier, Laurie, and Carole Simon-Smolinski. *Idaho's Ethnic Heritage: Historical Overviews*. 2 vols. Boise: Idaho Ethnic Heritage Project, 1990.

Tsurutani, Hisashi. *America-Bound: The Japanese and the Opening of the American West*. Translated by Betsey Scheiner. Tokyo: Japan Times, 1989.

Waite, Thornton. "On the Main Line at Last." *The Streamliner*, Union Pacific Historical Society, 11, no. 6.

Opposite: Livery stable on Bannock at 9th, about 1930
Next Page: Migrant farm boy in an FSA work camp, 1936

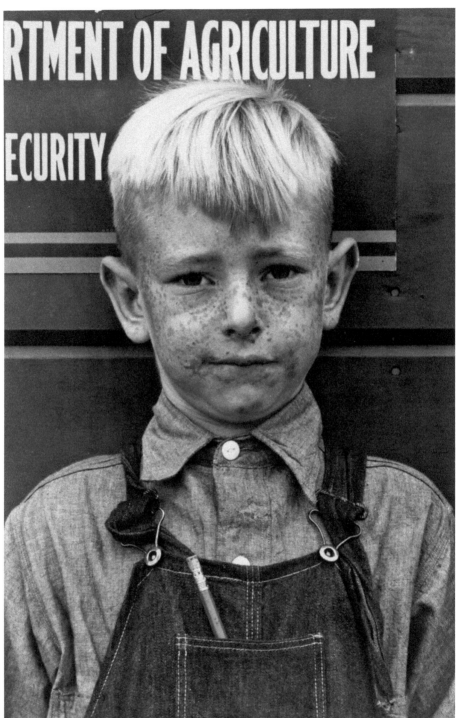

Walz, Eric. *Nikkei in the Interior West: Japanese Immigration and Community Building, 1882-1945*. Tucson: University of Arizona Press, 2012.

Wilson, Robert Arden, and Bill Hosokawa. *East to America: A History of the Japanese in the United States*. New York: Morrow, 1980.

Chapter 3: Unfit for Habitation

An Act to Provide for the Care of the Poor in Ada County. Passed by the Fourteenth Session of the Legislative Assembly, February 8, 1883, Remaining in Force, June 1, 1887.

An Act to Provide for the Indigent Insane in the Territory of Idaho. Passed by the Eleventh Session of the Territorial Legislature, 1881.

Clement, Priscilla Ferguson. *Welfare and the Poor in the Nineteenth-Century City*. Rutherford, NJ: Fairleigh Dickinson University Press, 1985.

Haber, Carole. "'And the Fear of the Poorhouse': Perceptions of Old Age Impoverishment in Early Twentieth-Century America." *Generations* 17, no. 2 (1993): 46-49.

Hart, Arthur. *The Boise Children's Home: A History*. Boise: Children's Home Society of Idaho, 1996.

Idaho Statesman, 1883-1884, 1891-1895, 1915-1916, 1944, 1949.

Katz, Michael B. *In the Shadow of the Poorhouse: A Social History of Welfare in America*. New York: Basic Books, 1986.

MacGregor, Carol. *Boise, Idaho, 1882-1910: Prosperity in Isolation*. Missoula, MT: Mountain Press, 2006.

Selmi, Patrick. "The Poorhouse: America's Forgotten Institution." *Journal of Progressive Human Services* 19, no. 2 (2008): 172-175.

Sermon, Susan. "'Beyond Simple Domesticity': Organizing Boise Women, 1866-1920." Master's thesis, Boise State University, 1996.

Wagner, David. *The Poorhouse: America's Forgotten Institution*. Lanham, MD: Rowan & Littlefield, 2005.

Chapter 4: Hammer and Drill

Bell, Robert N. "Seventh Annual Report of the Mining Industry of Idaho for the Year 1905." State of Idaho, State Inspector of Mines, no. 7 (1906): 35-37.

Bell, Robert N. "Eighth Annual Report of the Mining Industry of Idaho for the Year 1905." State of Idaho, State Inspector Mines, no. 8 (1907): 40-43.

Bell, Robert N. "Pearl Mining District, Once Abandoned, Now Booming." *Capital News* (Boise), August 31, 1935.

Idaho State Historical Society. "Mining in Idaho." Idaho State Historical Society Reference Series, no. 9, 1985.

Miller, Donald. " America 1900: The Dangers of Mining." *American Experience* documentary series, Public Broadcasting Service, 2006. http://www.pbs.org/wgbh/amex/1900/filmmore/reference/interview/miller_dangersofmining.html

Moore, F. Cushing. "Twelfth Annual Report of the Mining Industry of Idaho for the Year 1910." Weiser, ID: Signal Company, 1911.

State of Idaho, Department of Environmental Quality. "Lincoln Mine Preliminary Assessment Report, Gem County, Idaho." Boise: State of Idaho, Department of Environmental Quality, October 2003.

Waldemar, Lindgren. "The Mining District of the Idaho Basin and Boise Ridge, Idaho." USGS 18th Annual Report, Part III (1898): 619-719.

Weldin, Robert. "The Rise and Demise of a Historic Mining Site." *Mining History News* 16, no. 4 (2005): 1-7.

Chapter 5: Razing Levy's Alley

Baertsch, Blaine. "Boise Officials, VIPs Dedicate New City Hall." *Idaho Statesman*, March 16, 1977.

"Boise Urban Renewal Project Map." Capital City Development Corporation Public Records, Box 7, Appraisals, Project Area 1, Document no. 28.

"Commercial Sites and Sales Listings." Capital City Development Corporation Public Records, Box 7, Appraisals, Project Area 1, Document no. 24.

Hart, Arthur. "'Frail Sisterhood' Contributed to City." *Idaho Statesman*, August 6, 1973.

Hart, Arthur. "Levy's Alley Recalled." *Idaho Statesman*, September 2, 1973.

Idaho Statesman, 1892-1897.

Pitman, Alina Lynn. "The Unwanted Desired: Boise's Attempt to Contain Prostitution in the 1970s." Master's thesis, Boise State University, 2006.

"Practical Pharmacology: The Heavy Metals and Their Salts." *Journal of the American Medical Association* 65, no. 3 (1915): 247-251.

Russell, Jo Anne. "A Necessary Evil: Prostitutes, Patriarchs & Profits in Boise City, 1863-1915." Master's thesis, Boise State University, 1991.

Woodward, Tim. "Levy's Alley 'Lights Up' Again in Dispute with Highway District." *Idaho Statesman*, February 22, 1974.

Zarkin, David. "Government of Boise Outgrows City Hall in 31 Years since Construction by WPA." *Idaho Statesman*, August 15, 1969.

Chapter 6: Women Behind Bars

Beierle, Amber, Ashley Phillips, and Hanako Wakatsuki. *Images of America: Old Idaho Penitentiary*. Mt. Pleasant, SC: Arcadia Publishing, 2014.

Idaho State Historical Society. Public Archives and Research Library. Idaho Penitentiary Inmates 1864-1947: Catalog–Women.

Idaho Statesman, 1870, 1884, 1903, 1949, 1960, 1963.

Kendrick, Katie (Compiler).The Old Idaho State Penitentiary: Female State Biographies. Research compiled by Boise State University, 2010-2011.

Rafter, Nicole Hahn. "Prisons for Women, 1790-1980." *Crime and Justice* 5 (1983): 129-181.

Stacy, Susan. "'Our Ward Is Rather Small.'" *Idaho Yesterdays* 38, no. 2 (1994): 22.

Waite, Robert. "Necessary to Isolate the Female Prisoners: Women Convicts and the Women's Ward at the Old Idaho Penitentiary." *Idaho Yesterdays* 29, no. 3 (1985): 2-15.

Chapter 7: God and Reclamation

Arrington, Leonard. "The New Deal in the West: A Preliminary Statistical Inquiry." *Pacific Historical Review* 38, no. 3 (1969): 311-316.

"Boise Project History, 1920-1945." Idaho State Historical Society Reference Series 193: 1-5.

"Canyon County Claims the Largest Government Irrigation Project So Far Built in the United States." *Capital News* (Boise), January 3, 1926.

Gahan, Andrew H., and William D. Rowley. *The Bureau of Reclamation: From Developing to Managing Water, 1945-2000*. Vol. 2. Denver, CO: U.S. Department of the Interior, Bureau of Reclamation, 2012.

Lorimer, Bob. "Water Brought Prosperity to Little Village." *Idaho Statesman*, April 24, 1966.

Malone, Michael P. "The New Deal in Idaho." *Pacific Historical Review* 38, no. 3 (1969): 293-310.

Montgomery, Richard Calvin. "Canyon County: The Economic Geography of a Southwestern Idaho Irrigated Area." Master's thesis, University of Nebraska, 1951.

Morgan, Jane. "Failure on the Boise Project, 1905-1924." *Idaho Yesterdays* 50, no. 1 (2009): 32-40.

Mutch, Donald B. Oral history (OH #0530) interview by John Mutch, March 9, 1980. Boise: Idaho State Archives and Research Center, Oral History Collection.

Robinson, Michael C. *Water for the West: The Bureau of Reclamation, 1902-1977*. Chicago: Public Works Historical Society, 1979.

Tonsfeldt, Ward, and Paul G. Claeyssens. "Pre-industrial Period: 1870-1910: Irrigation." Oregon History Project. Portland: Oregon Historical Society Museum and Research Library, 2004.

Chapter 8: Nazis on the Homefront

Harper, Wayne. "Project: Emmett Fruit Industry." Interview by Amy McBryde, January 23, 1988. Boise: Idaho State Archives and Research Center, Oral History Collection.

Jaehn, Tomas. "Unlikely Harvesters: German Prisoners of War as Agricultural Workers in the Northwest." *Montana: The Magazine of Western History* 50, no. 3 (2000): 46-57.

Kirkpatrick, Kathy. *Prisoner of War Camps across America*. Salt Lake City, UT: GenTracer, 2012.

Krammer, Arnold. *Nazi Prisoners of War in America*. Lanham, MD: Scarborough House, 1979.

"Labor Supply Center Adopts Working Rules." *Idaho Statesman*, April 28, 1945.

Miller, Wendy. "Prisoner of War Camps in Idaho." In *A Little of This, a Little of That, an Anthology*, edited by Larry Cain. Nampa, ID: Larry Cain for the Canyon County Historical Society, 2010.

Naher, Albert. Oral history interview by Tomas Jaehn, January 11, 1994, August 4, 1995. Boise: Idaho State Archives and Research Center, Oral History Collection.

National Archives and Records Service. Records of the Office of Provost Marshal General, 1941-1975, Record Group 389. "Suggestions for Thinning and Blocking Sugar Beets." NND770123. U.S. Military, 1945.

"U.S. Contract with Labor Group Expires; Prisoners to Work in Beet Fields Next Week Despite Deadline." *Idaho Statesman*, November 16, 1945.

Chapter 9: South of the Tracks

Alegria, Henry. *75 Years of Memoirs*. Caldwell, ID: Caxton Printers, 1981.

Bieter, John, and Mark Bieter. *An Enduring Legacy: The Story of Basques in Idaho*. Reno: University of Nevada Press, 2000.

Davis, Lawrence J. "Tearing Down Boise." *Harpers* 249 (1974): 32-45.

Idaho Black History Museum. *History of Blacks in Idaho*. Boise: Idaho Black History Museum, 2004.

Idaho Black History Museum. *The Invisible Idahoan: 200 Years of Blacks in Idaho, Part 2: The Black Idahoan in Transition, 1920-1968*. Boise: Idaho Black History Museum, 2005.

Idaho Black History Museum. *The Invisible Idahoan: 200 Years of Blacks in Idaho, Part 3: The Enduring Presence and Contributions of Black Idahoans, 1969-2006*. Boise: Idaho Black History Museum, 2006.

Johns, Jeffrey D. "The River Street Neighborhood." Unpublished manuscript, Boise State University, 1995.

Oliver, Mamie O. 2001. *Blacks in Idaho's White Press: 1863-1916*. Littleton, CO: Thornton Publishing.

Osa, Mateo. "Lee Street Historic District: Survey of Lee Street Neighborhood Project Summary, Boise." Manuscript no. 93. Boise: Idaho Oral History Center/Idaho State Historical Society, 1981.

Stacy, Susan M. "River Street Area Survey 1995: Survey Overview." Prepared for the City of Boise and the Capital City Development Corporation, Boise, ID, 1995.

Chapter 10: Hard Times at Chula Vista

Blough, Dorris. "The Monkeys Have It Better than the Migrants." *Intermountain Observer* (Boise), August 7, 1971.

Caufield, Celine. "History of the Hispanic Ministry of the Roman Catholic Diocese of Boise." Files of the Multicultural Ministry of the Roman Catholic Diocese of Boise, Box 8, May 1989.

Franklin, Marcia (Producer). Interview with former Idaho governor Phil Batt. *The Color of Conscience* documentary series, Idaho Public Television, 2011. http://idahoptv.org/productions/specials/colorofconscience/philbatt.cfm

Gamboa, Erasmo. *Mexican Labor and World War II: Braceros in the Pacific Northwest, 1942-1947*. Austin: University of Texas Press, 1990.

Idaho Governor's Migratory Labor Committee. "Reports on Idaho Migratory Labor Camps." Boise, ID: Migratory Labor Committee, 1955-1966.

Jones, Errol D. "Latinos in Idaho: Making Their Way in the Gem State." In *Idaho's Place: A New History of the Gem State*, edited by Adam M. Soward, 201-237. Seattle: University of Washington Press, 2014.

Peterson, Robin. "Idaho Migrant Labor Camps, 1930-1980." Master's thesis, Boise State University, 2000.

Planas, Roque. "A Tiny Rural Town Just Elected an All-Latino City Council." *HuffPost*, Dec. 1, 2015. http://www.huffingtonpost.com/entry/latino-city-council-idaho_us_565cd443e4b08e945fec5701

Schwantes, Carlos A. *In Mountain Shadows: A History of Idaho*. Lincoln: University of Nebraska Press, 1991.

9 780990 736349